C-4488 CAREER EXAMINATION SERIES

This is your
PASSBOOK for...

Port Authority Electrician

Test Preparation Study Guide
Questions & Answers

NATIONAL LEARNING CORPORATION®

COPYRIGHT NOTICE

This book is SOLELY intended for, is sold ONLY to, and its use is RESTRICTED to individual, bona fide applicants or candidates who qualify by virtue of having seriously filed applications for appropriate license, certificate, professional and/or promotional advancement, higher school matriculation, scholarship, or other legitimate requirements of education and/or governmental authorities.

This book is NOT intended for use, class instruction, tutoring, training, duplication, copying, reprinting, excerption, or adaptation, etc., by:

1) Other publishers
2) Proprietors and/or Instructors of "Coaching" and/or Preparatory Courses
3) Personnel and/or Training Divisions of commercial, industrial, and governmental organizations
4) Schools, colleges, or universities and/or their departments and staffs, including teachers and other personnel
5) Testing Agencies or Bureaus
6) Study groups which seek by the purchase of a single volume to copy and/or duplicate and/or adapt this material for use by the group as a whole without having purchased individual volumes for each of the members of the group
7) Et al.

Such persons would be in violation of appropriate Federal and State statutes.

PROVISION OF LICENSING AGREEMENTS – Recognized educational, commercial, industrial, and governmental institutions and organizations, and others legitimately engaged in educational pursuits, including training, testing, and measurement activities, may address request for a licensing agreement to the copyright owners, who will determine whether, and under what conditions, including fees and charges, the materials in this book may be used them. In other words, a licensing facility exists for the legitimate use of the material in this book on other than an individual basis. However, it is asseverated and affirmed here that the material in this book CANNOT be used without the receipt of the express permission of such a licensing agreement from the Publishers. Inquiries re licensing should be addressed to the company, attention rights and permissions department.

All rights reserved, including the right of reproduction in whole or in part, in any form or by any means, electronic or mechanical, including photocopying, recording, or by any information storage and retrieval system, without permission in writing from the Publisher.

Copyright © 2024 by
National Learning Corporation

212 Michael Drive, Syosset, NY 11791
(516) 921-8888 • www.passbooks.com
E-mail: info@passbooks.com

PUBLISHED IN THE UNITED STATES OF AMERICA

PASSBOOK® SERIES

THE *PASSBOOK® SERIES* has been created to prepare applicants and candidates for the ultimate academic battlefield – the examination room.

At some time in our lives, each and every one of us may be required to take an examination – for validation, matriculation, admission, qualification, registration, certification, or licensure.

Based on the assumption that every applicant or candidate has met the basic formal educational standards, has taken the required number of courses, and read the necessary texts, the *PASSBOOK® SERIES* furnishes the one special preparation which may assure passing with confidence, instead of failing with insecurity. Examination questions – together with answers – are furnished as the basic vehicle for study so that the mysteries of the examination and its compounding difficulties may be eliminated or diminished by a sure method.

This book is meant to help you pass your examination provided that you qualify and are serious in your objective.

The entire field is reviewed through the huge store of content information which is succinctly presented through a provocative and challenging approach – the question-and-answer method.

A climate of success is established by furnishing the correct answers at the end of each test.

You soon learn to recognize types of questions, forms of questions, and patterns of questioning. You may even begin to anticipate expected outcomes.

You perceive that many questions are repeated or adapted so that you can gain acute insights, which may enable you to score many sure points.

You learn how to confront new questions, or types of questions, and to attack them confidently and work out the correct answers.

You note objectives and emphases, and recognize pitfalls and dangers, so that you may make positive educational adjustments.

Moreover, you are kept fully informed in relation to new concepts, methods, practices, and directions in the field.

You discover that you are actually taking the examination all the time: you are preparing for the examination by "taking" an examination, not by reading extraneous and/or supererogatory textbooks.

In short, this PASSBOOK®, used directedly, should be an important factor in helping you to pass your test.

PORT AUTHORITY ELECTRICIAN

DUTIES
The Port Authority Electrician performs journey-level installation, maintenance, and repair to various electrical equipment, such as: generators, motors, fire alarm systems, toll equipment, traffic signals, control boxes and automatic electrical systems. The Electrician works from schematic drawings, blueprints or rough sketches and may splice cables, install conduit, BX cable and similar types of electrical wiring. The Electrician is required to work at elevated heights from ladders and bucket trucks and may lead one or more electrical helpers.

SCOPE OF THE EXAMINATION
The written Examination is designed to test knowledge/ability in the following areas:
1. Electrical Theory;
2. National Electrical Code;
3. Transformers;
4. Motors;
5. Controllers; and
6. Basic Electronics.

HOW TO TAKE A TEST

I. YOU MUST PASS AN EXAMINATION

A. *WHAT EVERY CANDIDATE SHOULD KNOW*

Examination applicants often ask us for help in preparing for the written test. What can I study in advance? What kinds of questions will be asked? How will the test be given? How will the papers be graded?

As an applicant for a civil service examination, you may be wondering about some of these things. Our purpose here is to suggest effective methods of advance study and to describe civil service examinations.

Your chances for success on this examination can be increased if you know how to prepare. Those "pre-examination jitters" can be reduced if you know what to expect. You can even experience an adventure in good citizenship if you know why civil service exams are given.

B. *WHY ARE CIVIL SERVICE EXAMINATIONS GIVEN?*

Civil service examinations are important to you in two ways. As a citizen, you want public jobs filled by employees who know how to do their work. As a job seeker, you want a fair chance to compete for that job on an equal footing with other candidates. The best-known means of accomplishing this two-fold goal is the competitive examination.

Exams are widely publicized throughout the nation. They may be administered for jobs in federal, state, city, municipal, town or village governments or agencies.

Any citizen may apply, with some limitations, such as the age or residence of applicants. Your experience and education may be reviewed to see whether you meet the requirements for the particular examination. When these requirements exist, they are reasonable and applied consistently to all applicants. Thus, a competitive examination may cause you some uneasiness now, but it is your privilege and safeguard.

C. *HOW ARE CIVIL SERVICE EXAMS DEVELOPED?*

Examinations are carefully written by trained technicians who are specialists in the field known as "psychological measurement," in consultation with recognized authorities in the field of work that the test will cover. These experts recommend the subject matter areas or skills to be tested; only those knowledges or skills important to your success on the job are included. The most reliable books and source materials available are used as references. Together, the experts and technicians judge the difficulty level of the questions.

Test technicians know how to phrase questions so that the problem is clearly stated. Their ethics do not permit "trick" or "catch" questions. Questions may have been tried out on sample groups, or subjected to statistical analysis, to determine their usefulness.

Written tests are often used in combination with performance tests, ratings of training and experience, and oral interviews. All of these measures combine to form the best-known means of finding the right person for the right job.

II. HOW TO PASS THE WRITTEN TEST

A. NATURE OF THE EXAMINATION

To prepare intelligently for civil service examinations, you should know how they differ from school examinations you have taken. In school you were assigned certain definite pages to read or subjects to cover. The examination questions were quite detailed and usually emphasized memory. Civil service exams, on the other hand, try to discover your present ability to perform the duties of a position, plus your potentiality to learn these duties. In other words, a civil service exam attempts to predict how successful you will be. Questions cover such a broad area that they cannot be as minute and detailed as school exam questions.

In the public service similar kinds of work, or positions, are grouped together in one "class." This process is known as *position-classification*. All the positions in a class are paid according to the salary range for that class. One class title covers all of these positions, and they are all tested by the same examination.

B. FOUR BASIC STEPS

1) Study the announcement

How, then, can you know what subjects to study? Our best answer is: "Learn as much as possible about the class of positions for which you've applied." The exam will test the knowledge, skills and abilities needed to do the work.

Your most valuable source of information about the position you want is the official exam announcement. This announcement lists the training and experience qualifications. Check these standards and apply only if you come reasonably close to meeting them.

The brief description of the position in the examination announcement offers some clues to the subjects which will be tested. Think about the job itself. Review the duties in your mind. Can you perform them, or are there some in which you are rusty? Fill in the blank spots in your preparation.

Many jurisdictions preview the written test in the exam announcement by including a section called "Knowledge and Abilities Required," "Scope of the Examination," or some similar heading. Here you will find out specifically what fields will be tested.

2) Review your own background

Once you learn in general what the position is all about, and what you need to know to do the work, ask yourself which subjects you already know fairly well and which need improvement. You may wonder whether to concentrate on improving your strong areas or on building some background in your fields of weakness. When the announcement has specified "some knowledge" or "considerable knowledge," or has used adjectives like "beginning principles of..." or "advanced ... methods," you can get a clue as to the number and difficulty of questions to be asked in any given field. More questions, and hence broader coverage, would be included for those subjects which are more important in the work. Now weigh your strengths and weaknesses against the job requirements and prepare accordingly.

3) Determine the level of the position

Another way to tell how intensively you should prepare is to understand the level of the job for which you are applying. Is it the entering level? In other words, is this the position in which beginners in a field of work are hired? Or is it an intermediate or advanced level? Sometimes this is indicated by such words as "Junior" or "Senior" in the class title. Other jurisdictions use Roman numerals to designate the level – Clerk I, Clerk II, for example. The word "Supervisor" sometimes appears in the title. If the level is not indicated by the title, check the description of duties. Will you be working under very close supervision, or will you have responsibility for independent decisions in this work?

4) Choose appropriate study materials

Now that you know the subjects to be examined and the relative amount of each subject to be covered, you can choose suitable study materials. For beginning level jobs, or even advanced ones, if you have a pronounced weakness in some aspect of your training, read a modern, standard textbook in that field. Be sure it is up to date and has general coverage. Such books are normally available at your library, and the librarian will be glad to help you locate one. For entry-level positions, questions of appropriate difficulty are chosen – neither highly advanced questions, nor those too simple. Such questions require careful thought but not advanced training.

If the position for which you are applying is technical or advanced, you will read more advanced, specialized material. If you are already familiar with the basic principles of your field, elementary textbooks would waste your time. Concentrate on advanced textbooks and technical periodicals. Think through the concepts and review difficult problems in your field.

These are all general sources. You can get more ideas on your own initiative, following these leads. For example, training manuals and publications of the government agency which employs workers in your field can be useful, particularly for technical and professional positions. A letter or visit to the government department involved may result in more specific study suggestions, and certainly will provide you with a more definite idea of the exact nature of the position you are seeking.

III. KINDS OF TESTS

Tests are used for purposes other than measuring knowledge and ability to perform specified duties. For some positions, it is equally important to test ability to make adjustments to new situations or to profit from training. In others, basic mental abilities not dependent on information are essential. Questions which test these things may not appear as pertinent to the duties of the position as those which test for knowledge and information. Yet they are often highly important parts of a fair examination. For very general questions, it is almost impossible to help you direct your study efforts. What we can do is to point out some of the more common of these general abilities needed in public service positions and describe some typical questions.

1) General information

Broad, general information has been found useful for predicting job success in some kinds of work. This is tested in a variety of ways, from vocabulary lists to questions about current events. Basic background in some field of work, such as sociology or economics, may be sampled in a group of questions. Often these are principles which have become familiar to most persons through exposure rather than through formal training. It is difficult to advise you how to study for these questions; being alert to the world around you is our best suggestion.

2) Verbal ability

An example of an ability needed in many positions is verbal or language ability. Verbal ability is, in brief, the ability to use and understand words. Vocabulary and grammar tests are typical measures of this ability. Reading comprehension or paragraph interpretation questions are common in many kinds of civil service tests. You are given a paragraph of written material and asked to find its central meaning.

3) Numerical ability

Number skills can be tested by the familiar arithmetic problem, by checking paired lists of numbers to see which are alike and which are different, or by interpreting charts and graphs. In the latter test, a graph may be printed in the test booklet which you are asked to use as the basis for answering questions.

4) Observation

A popular test for law-enforcement positions is the observation test. A picture is shown to you for several minutes, then taken away. Questions about the picture test your ability to observe both details and larger elements.

5) Following directions

In many positions in the public service, the employee must be able to carry out written instructions dependably and accurately. You may be given a chart with several columns, each column listing a variety of information. The questions require you to carry out directions involving the information given in the chart.

6) Skills and aptitudes

Performance tests effectively measure some manual skills and aptitudes. When the skill is one in which you are trained, such as typing or shorthand, you can practice. These tests are often very much like those given in business school or high school courses. For many of the other skills and aptitudes, however, no short-time preparation can be made. Skills and abilities natural to you or that you have developed throughout your lifetime are being tested.

Many of the general questions just described provide all the data needed to answer the questions and ask you to use your reasoning ability to find the answers. Your best preparation for these tests, as well as for tests of facts and ideas, is to be at your physical and mental best. You, no doubt, have your own methods of getting into an exam-taking mood and keeping "in shape." The next section lists some ideas on this subject.

IV. KINDS OF QUESTIONS

Only rarely is the "essay" question, which you answer in narrative form, used in civil service tests. Civil service tests are usually of the short-answer type. Full instructions for answering these questions will be given to you at the examination. But in case this is your first experience with short-answer questions and separate answer sheets, here is what you need to know:

1) Multiple-choice Questions

Most popular of the short-answer questions is the "multiple choice" or "best answer" question. It can be used, for example, to test for factual knowledge, ability to solve problems or judgment in meeting situations found at work.

A multiple-choice question is normally one of three types—
- It can begin with an incomplete statement followed by several possible endings. You are to find the one ending which *best* completes the statement, although some of the others may not be entirely wrong.
- It can also be a complete statement in the form of a question which is answered by choosing one of the statements listed.

- It can be in the form of a problem – again you select the best answer.

Here is an example of a multiple-choice question with a discussion which should give you some clues as to the method for choosing the right answer:

When an employee has a complaint about his assignment, the action which will *best* help him overcome his difficulty is to
  A. discuss his difficulty with his coworkers
  B. take the problem to the head of the organization
  C. take the problem to the person who gave him the assignment
  D. say nothing to anyone about his complaint

In answering this question, you should study each of the choices to find which is best. Consider choice "A" – Certainly an employee may discuss his complaint with fellow employees, but no change or improvement can result, and the complaint remains unresolved. Choice "B" is a poor choice since the head of the organization probably does not know what assignment you have been given, and taking your problem to him is known as "going over the head" of the supervisor. The supervisor, or person who made the assignment, is the person who can clarify it or correct any injustice. Choice "C" is, therefore, correct. To say nothing, as in choice "D," is unwise. Supervisors have and interest in knowing the problems employees are facing, and the employee is seeking a solution to his problem.

2) True/False Questions

The "true/false" or "right/wrong" form of question is sometimes used. Here a complete statement is given. Your job is to decide whether the statement is right or wrong.

SAMPLE: A roaming cell-phone call to a nearby city costs less than a non-roaming call to a distant city.

This statement is wrong, or false, since roaming calls are more expensive.

This is not a complete list of all possible question forms, although most of the others are variations of these common types. You will always get complete directions for answering questions. Be sure you understand *how* to mark your answers – ask questions until you do.

V. RECORDING YOUR ANSWERS

Computer terminals are used more and more today for many different kinds of exams.

For an examination with very few applicants, you may be told to record your answers in the test booklet itself. Separate answer sheets are much more common. If this separate answer sheet is to be scored by machine – and this is often the case – it is highly important that you mark your answers correctly in order to get credit.

An electronic scoring machine is often used in civil service offices because of the speed with which papers can be scored. Machine-scored answer sheets must be marked with a pencil, which will be given to you. This pencil has a high graphite content which responds to the electronic scoring machine. As a matter of fact, stray dots may register as answers, so do not let your pencil rest on the answer sheet while you are pondering the correct answer. Also, if your pencil lead breaks or is otherwise defective, ask for another.

Since the answer sheet will be dropped in a slot in the scoring machine, be careful not to bend the corners or get the paper crumpled.

The answer sheet normally has five vertical columns of numbers, with 30 numbers to a column. These numbers correspond to the question numbers in your test booklet. After each number, going across the page are four or five pairs of dotted lines. These short dotted lines have small letters or numbers above them. The first two pairs may also have a "T" or "F" above the letters. This indicates that the first two pairs only are to be used if the questions are of the true-false type. If the questions are multiple choice, disregard the "T" and "F" and pay attention only to the small letters or numbers.

Answer your questions in the manner of the sample that follows:

32. The largest city in the United States is
    A. Washington, D.C.
    B. New York City
    C. Chicago
    D. Detroit
    E. San Francisco

1) Choose the answer you think is best. (New York City is the largest, so "B" is correct.)
2) Find the row of dotted lines numbered the same as the question you are answering. (Find row number 32)
3) Find the pair of dotted lines corresponding to the answer. (Find the pair of lines under the mark "B.")
4) Make a solid black mark between the dotted lines.

VI. BEFORE THE TEST

Common sense will help you find procedures to follow to get ready for an examination. Too many of us, however, overlook these sensible measures. Indeed, nervousness and fatigue have been found to be the most serious reasons why applicants fail to do their best on civil service tests. Here is a list of reminders:

- Begin your preparation early – Don't wait until the last minute to go scurrying around for books and materials or to find out what the position is all about.
- Prepare continuously – An hour a night for a week is better than an all-night cram session. This has been definitely established. What is more, a night a week for a month will return better dividends than crowding your study into a shorter period of time.
- Locate the place of the exam – You have been sent a notice telling you when and where to report for the examination. If the location is in a different town or otherwise unfamiliar to you, it would be well to inquire the best route and learn something about the building.
- Relax the night before the test – Allow your mind to rest. Do not study at all that night. Plan some mild recreation or diversion; then go to bed early and get a good night's sleep.
- Get up early enough to make a leisurely trip to the place for the test – This way unforeseen events, traffic snarls, unfamiliar buildings, etc. will not upset you.
- Dress comfortably – A written test is not a fashion show. You will be known by number and not by name, so wear something comfortable.

- Leave excess paraphernalia at home – Shopping bags and odd bundles will get in your way. You need bring only the items mentioned in the official notice you received; usually everything you need is provided. Do not bring reference books to the exam. They will only confuse those last minutes and be taken away from you when in the test room.
- Arrive somewhat ahead of time – If because of transportation schedules you must get there very early, bring a newspaper or magazine to take your mind off yourself while waiting.
- Locate the examination room – When you have found the proper room, you will be directed to the seat or part of the room where you will sit. Sometimes you are given a sheet of instructions to read while you are waiting. Do not fill out any forms until you are told to do so; just read them and be prepared.
- Relax and prepare to listen to the instructions
- If you have any physical problem that may keep you from doing your best, be sure to tell the test administrator. If you are sick or in poor health, you really cannot do your best on the exam. You can come back and take the test some other time.

VII. AT THE TEST

The day of the test is here and you have the test booklet in your hand. The temptation to get going is very strong. Caution! There is more to success than knowing the right answers. You must know how to identify your papers and understand variations in the type of short-answer question used in this particular examination. Follow these suggestions for maximum results from your efforts:

1) Cooperate with the monitor

The test administrator has a duty to create a situation in which you can be as much at ease as possible. He will give instructions, tell you when to begin, check to see that you are marking your answer sheet correctly, and so on. He is not there to guard you, although he will see that your competitors do not take unfair advantage. He wants to help you do your best.

2) Listen to all instructions

Don't jump the gun! Wait until you understand all directions. In most civil service tests you get more time than you need to answer the questions. So don't be in a hurry. Read each word of instructions until you clearly understand the meaning. Study the examples, listen to all announcements and follow directions. Ask questions if you do not understand what to do.

3) Identify your papers

Civil service exams are usually identified by number only. You will be assigned a number; you must not put your name on your test papers. Be sure to copy your number correctly. Since more than one exam may be given, copy your exact examination title.

4) Plan your time

Unless you are told that a test is a "speed" or "rate of work" test, speed itself is usually not important. Time enough to answer all the questions will be provided, but this does not mean that you have all day. An overall time limit has been set. Divide the total time (in minutes) by the number of questions to determine the approximate time you have for each question.

5) Do not linger over difficult questions

If you come across a difficult question, mark it with a paper clip (useful to have along) and come back to it when you have been through the booklet. One caution if you do this – be sure to skip a number on your answer sheet as well. Check often to be sure that you have not lost your place and that you are marking in the row numbered the same as the question you are answering.

6) Read the questions

Be sure you know what the question asks! Many capable people are unsuccessful because they failed to *read* the questions correctly.

7) Answer all questions

Unless you have been instructed that a penalty will be deducted for incorrect answers, it is better to guess than to omit a question.

8) Speed tests

It is often better NOT to guess on speed tests. It has been found that on timed tests people are tempted to spend the last few seconds before time is called in marking answers at random – without even reading them – in the hope of picking up a few extra points. To discourage this practice, the instructions may warn you that your score will be "corrected" for guessing. That is, a penalty will be applied. The incorrect answers will be deducted from the correct ones, or some other penalty formula will be used.

9) Review your answers

If you finish before time is called, go back to the questions you guessed or omitted to give them further thought. Review other answers if you have time.

10) Return your test materials

If you are ready to leave before others have finished or time is called, take ALL your materials to the monitor and leave quietly. Never take any test material with you. The monitor can discover whose papers are not complete, and taking a test booklet may be grounds for disqualification.

VIII. EXAMINATION TECHNIQUES

1) Read the general instructions carefully. These are usually printed on the first page of the exam booklet. As a rule, these instructions refer to the timing of the examination; the fact that you should not start work until the signal and must stop work at a signal, etc. If there are any *special* instructions, such as a choice of questions to be answered, make sure that you note this instruction carefully.

2) When you are ready to start work on the examination, that is as soon as the signal has been given, read the instructions to each question booklet, underline any key words or phrases, such as *least, best, outline, describe* and the like. In this way you will tend to answer as requested rather than discover on reviewing your paper that you *listed without describing*, that you selected the *worst* choice rather than the *best* choice, etc.

3) If the examination is of the objective or multiple-choice type – that is, each question will also give a series of possible answers: A, B, C or D, and you are called upon to select the best answer and write the letter next to that answer on your answer paper – it is advisable to start answering each question in turn. There may be anywhere from 50 to 100 such questions in the three or four hours allotted and you can see how much time would be taken if you read through all the questions before beginning to answer any. Furthermore, if you come across a question or group of questions which you know would be difficult to answer, it would undoubtedly affect your handling of all the other questions.

4) If the examination is of the essay type and contains but a few questions, it is a moot point as to whether you should read all the questions before starting to answer any one. Of course, if you are given a choice – say five out of seven and the like – then it is essential to read all the questions so you can eliminate the two that are most difficult. If, however, you are asked to answer all the questions, there may be danger in trying to answer the easiest one first because you may find that you will spend too much time on it. The best technique is to answer the first question, then proceed to the second, etc.

5) Time your answers. Before the exam begins, write down the time it started, then add the time allowed for the examination and write down the time it must be completed, then divide the time available somewhat as follows:
   - If 3-1/2 hours are allowed, that would be 210 minutes. If you have 80 objective-type questions, that would be an average of 2-1/2 minutes per question. Allow yourself no more than 2 minutes per question, or a total of 160 minutes, which will permit about 50 minutes to review.
   - If for the time allotment of 210 minutes there are 7 essay questions to answer, that would average about 30 minutes a question. Give yourself only 25 minutes per question so that you have about 35 minutes to review.

6) The most important instruction is to *read each question* and make sure you know what is wanted. The second most important instruction is to *time yourself properly* so that you answer every question. The third most important instruction is to *answer every question*. Guess if you have to but include something for each question. Remember that you will receive no credit for a blank and will probably receive some credit if you write something in answer to an essay question. If you guess a letter – say "B" for a multiple-choice question – you may have guessed right. If you leave a blank as an answer to a multiple-choice question, the examiners may respect your feelings but it will not add a point to your score. Some exams may penalize you for wrong answers, so in such cases *only*, you may not want to guess unless you have some basis for your answer.

7) Suggestions
   a. Objective-type questions
      1. Examine the question booklet for proper sequence of pages and questions
      2. Read all instructions carefully
      3. Skip any question which seems too difficult; return to it after all other questions have been answered
      4. Apportion your time properly; do not spend too much time on any single question or group of questions

5. Note and underline key words – *all, most, fewest, least, best, worst, same, opposite,* etc.
6. Pay particular attention to negatives
7. Note unusual option, e.g., unduly long, short, complex, different or similar in content to the body of the question
8. Observe the use of "hedging" words – *probably, may, most likely,* etc.
9. Make sure that your answer is put next to the same number as the question
10. Do not second-guess unless you have good reason to believe the second answer is definitely more correct
11. Cross out original answer if you decide another answer is more accurate; do not erase until you are ready to hand your paper in
12. Answer all questions; guess unless instructed otherwise
13. Leave time for review

b. Essay questions
1. Read each question carefully
2. Determine exactly what is wanted. Underline key words or phrases.
3. Decide on outline or paragraph answer
4. Include many different points and elements unless asked to develop any one or two points or elements
5. Show impartiality by giving pros and cons unless directed to select one side only
6. Make and write down any assumptions you find necessary to answer the questions
7. Watch your English, grammar, punctuation and choice of words
8. Time your answers; don't crowd material

8) Answering the essay question

Most essay questions can be answered by framing the specific response around several key words or ideas. Here are a few such key words or ideas:

M's: manpower, materials, methods, money, management
P's: purpose, program, policy, plan, procedure, practice, problems, pitfalls, personnel, public relations

a. Six basic steps in handling problems:
1. Preliminary plan and background development
2. Collect information, data and facts
3. Analyze and interpret information, data and facts
4. Analyze and develop solutions as well as make recommendations
5. Prepare report and sell recommendations
6. Install recommendations and follow up effectiveness

b. Pitfalls to avoid
1. *Taking things for granted* – A statement of the situation does not necessarily imply that each of the elements is necessarily true; for example, a complaint may be invalid and biased so that all that can be taken for granted is that a complaint has been registered

2. *Considering only one side of a situation* – Wherever possible, indicate several alternatives and then point out the reasons you selected the best one
3. *Failing to indicate follow up* – Whenever your answer indicates action on your part, make certain that you will take proper follow-up action to see how successful your recommendations, procedures or actions turn out to be
4. *Taking too long in answering any single question* – Remember to time your answers properly

IX. AFTER THE TEST

Scoring procedures differ in detail among civil service jurisdictions although the general principles are the same. Whether the papers are hand-scored or graded by machine we have described, they are nearly always graded by number. That is, the person who marks the paper knows only the number – never the name – of the applicant. Not until all the papers have been graded will they be matched with names. If other tests, such as training and experience or oral interview ratings have been given, scores will be combined. Different parts of the examination usually have different weights. For example, the written test might count 60 percent of the final grade, and a rating of training and experience 40 percent. In many jurisdictions, veterans will have a certain number of points added to their grades.

After the final grade has been determined, the names are placed in grade order and an eligible list is established. There are various methods for resolving ties between those who get the same final grade – probably the most common is to place first the name of the person whose application was received first. Job offers are made from the eligible list in the order the names appear on it. You will be notified of your grade and your rank as soon as all these computations have been made. This will be done as rapidly as possible.

People who are found to meet the requirements in the announcement are called "eligibles." Their names are put on a list of eligible candidates. An eligible's chances of getting a job depend on how high he stands on this list and how fast agencies are filling jobs from the list.

When a job is to be filled from a list of eligibles, the agency asks for the names of people on the list of eligibles for that job. When the civil service commission receives this request, it sends to the agency the names of the three people highest on this list. Or, if the job to be filled has specialized requirements, the office sends the agency the names of the top three persons who meet these requirements from the general list.

The appointing officer makes a choice from among the three people whose names were sent to him. If the selected person accepts the appointment, the names of the others are put back on the list to be considered for future openings.

That is the rule in hiring from all kinds of eligible lists, whether they are for typist, carpenter, chemist, or something else. For every vacancy, the appointing officer has his choice of any one of the top three eligibles on the list. This explains why the person whose name is on top of the list sometimes does not get an appointment when some of the persons lower on the list do. If the appointing officer chooses the second or third eligible, the No. 1 eligible does not get a job at once, but stays on the list until he is appointed or the list is terminated.

X. HOW TO PASS THE INTERVIEW TEST

The examination for which you applied requires an oral interview test. You have already taken the written test and you are now being called for the interview test – the final part of the formal examination.

You may think that it is not possible to prepare for an interview test and that there are no procedures to follow during an interview. Our purpose is to point out some things you can do in advance that will help you and some good rules to follow and pitfalls to avoid while you are being interviewed.

What is an interview supposed to test?

The written examination is designed to test the technical knowledge and competence of the candidate; the oral is designed to evaluate intangible qualities, not readily measured otherwise, and to establish a list showing the relative fitness of each candidate – as measured against his competitors – for the position sought. Scoring is not on the basis of "right" and "wrong," but on a sliding scale of values ranging from "not passable" to "outstanding." As a matter of fact, it is possible to achieve a relatively low score without a single "incorrect" answer because of evident weakness in the qualities being measured.

Occasionally, an examination may consist entirely of an oral test – either an individual or a group oral. In such cases, information is sought concerning the technical knowledges and abilities of the candidate, since there has been no written examination for this purpose. More commonly, however, an oral test is used to supplement a written examination.

Who conducts interviews?

The composition of oral boards varies among different jurisdictions. In nearly all, a representative of the personnel department serves as chairman. One of the members of the board may be a representative of the department in which the candidate would work. In some cases, "outside experts" are used, and, frequently, a businessman or some other representative of the general public is asked to serve. Labor and management or other special groups may be represented. The aim is to secure the services of experts in the appropriate field.

However the board is composed, it is a good idea (and not at all improper or unethical) to ascertain in advance of the interview who the members are and what groups they represent. When you are introduced to them, you will have some idea of their backgrounds and interests, and at least you will not stutter and stammer over their names.

What should be done before the interview?

While knowledge about the board members is useful and takes some of the surprise element out of the interview, there is other preparation which is more substantive. It *is* possible to prepare for an oral interview – in several ways:

1) Keep a copy of your application and review it carefully before the interview

This may be the only document before the oral board, and the starting point of the interview. Know what education and experience you have listed there, and the sequence and dates of all of it. Sometimes the board will ask you to review the highlights of your experience for them; you should not have to hem and haw doing it.

2) Study the class specification and the examination announcement

Usually, the oral board has one or both of these to guide them. The qualities, characteristics or knowledges required by the position sought are stated in these documents. They offer valuable clues as to the nature of the oral interview. For example, if the job involves supervisory responsibilities, the announcement will usually indicate that knowledge of modern supervisory methods and the qualifications of the candidate as a supervisor will be tested. If so, you can expect such questions, frequently in the form of a hypothetical situation which you are expected to solve. NEVER go into an oral without knowledge of the duties and responsibilities of the job you seek.

3) Think through each qualification required

Try to visualize the kind of questions you would ask if you were a board member. How well could you answer them? Try especially to appraise your own knowledge and background in each area, *measured against the job sought*, and identify any areas in which you are weak. Be critical and realistic – do not flatter yourself.

4) Do some general reading in areas in which you feel you may be weak

For example, if the job involves supervision and your past experience has NOT, some general reading in supervisory methods and practices, particularly in the field of human relations, might be useful. Do NOT study agency procedures or detailed manuals. The oral board will be testing your understanding and capacity, not your memory.

5) Get a good night's sleep and watch your general health and mental attitude

You will want a clear head at the interview. Take care of a cold or any other minor ailment, and of course, no hangovers.

What should be done on the day of the interview?

Now comes the day of the interview itself. Give yourself plenty of time to get there. Plan to arrive somewhat ahead of the scheduled time, particularly if your appointment is in the fore part of the day. If a previous candidate fails to appear, the board might be ready for you a bit early. By early afternoon an oral board is almost invariably behind schedule if there are many candidates, and you may have to wait. Take along a book or magazine to read, or your application to review, but leave any extraneous material in the waiting room when you go in for your interview. In any event, relax and compose yourself.

The matter of dress is important. The board is forming impressions about you – from your experience, your manners, your attitude, and your appearance. Give your personal appearance careful attention. Dress your best, but not your flashiest. Choose conservative, appropriate clothing, and be sure it is immaculate. This is a business interview, and your appearance should indicate that you regard it as such. Besides, being well groomed and properly dressed will help boost your confidence.

Sooner or later, someone will call your name and escort you into the interview room. *This is it.* From here on you are on your own. It is too late for any more preparation. But remember, you asked for this opportunity to prove your fitness, and you are here because your request was granted.

What happens when you go in?

The usual sequence of events will be as follows: The clerk (who is often the board stenographer) will introduce you to the chairman of the oral board, who will introduce you to the other members of the board. Acknowledge the introductions before you sit down. Do not be surprised if you find a microphone facing you or a stenotypist sitting by. Oral interviews are usually recorded in the event of an appeal or other review.

Usually the chairman of the board will open the interview by reviewing the highlights of your education and work experience from your application – primarily for the benefit of the other members of the board, as well as to get the material into the record. Do not interrupt or comment unless there is an error or significant misinterpretation; if that is the case, do not hesitate. But do not quibble about insignificant matters. Also, he will usually ask you some question about your education, experience or your present job – partly to get you to start talking and to establish the interviewing "rapport." He may start the actual questioning, or turn it over to one of the other members. Frequently, each member undertakes the questioning on a particular area, one in which he is perhaps most competent, so you can expect each member to participate in the examination. Because time is limited, you may also expect some rather abrupt switches in the direction the questioning takes, so do not be upset by it. Normally, a board member will not pursue a single line of questioning unless he discovers a particular strength or weakness.

After each member has participated, the chairman will usually ask whether any member has any further questions, then will ask you if you have anything you wish to add. Unless you are expecting this question, it may floor you. Worse, it may start you off on an extended, extemporaneous speech. The board is not usually seeking more information. The question is principally to offer you a last opportunity to present further qualifications or to indicate that you have nothing to add. So, if you feel that a significant qualification or characteristic has been overlooked, it is proper to point it out in a sentence or so. Do not compliment the board on the thoroughness of their examination – they have been sketchy, and you know it. If you wish, merely say, "No thank you, I have nothing further to add." This is a point where you can "talk yourself out" of a good impression or fail to present an important bit of information. Remember, *you close the interview yourself.*

The chairman will then say, "That is all, Mr. _____, thank you." Do not be startled; the interview is over, and quicker than you think. Thank him, gather your belongings and take your leave. Save your sigh of relief for the other side of the door.

How to put your best foot forward

Throughout this entire process, you may feel that the board individually and collectively is trying to pierce your defenses, seek out your hidden weaknesses and embarrass and confuse you. Actually, this is not true. They are obliged to make an appraisal of your qualifications for the job you are seeking, and they want to see you in your best light. Remember, they must interview all candidates and a non-cooperative candidate may become a failure in spite of their best efforts to bring out his qualifications. Here are 15 suggestions that will help you:

1) Be natural – Keep your attitude confident, not cocky

If you are not confident that you can do the job, do not expect the board to be. Do not apologize for your weaknesses, try to bring out your strong points. The board is interested in a positive, not negative, presentation. Cockiness will antagonize any board member and make him wonder if you are covering up a weakness by a false show of strength.

2) Get comfortable, but don't lounge or sprawl

Sit erectly but not stiffly. A careless posture may lead the board to conclude that you are careless in other things, or at least that you are not impressed by the importance of the occasion. Either conclusion is natural, even if incorrect. Do not fuss with your clothing, a pencil or an ashtray. Your hands may occasionally be useful to emphasize a point; do not let them become a point of distraction.

3) Do not wisecrack or make small talk

This is a serious situation, and your attitude should show that you consider it as such. Further, the time of the board is limited – they do not want to waste it, and neither should you.

4) Do not exaggerate your experience or abilities

In the first place, from information in the application or other interviews and sources, the board may know more about you than you think. Secondly, you probably will not get away with it. An experienced board is rather adept at spotting such a situation, so do not take the chance.

5) If you know a board member, do not make a point of it, yet do not hide it

Certainly you are not fooling him, and probably not the other members of the board. Do not try to take advantage of your acquaintanceship – it will probably do you little good.

6) Do not dominate the interview

Let the board do that. They will give you the clues – do not assume that you have to do all the talking. Realize that the board has a number of questions to ask you, and do not try to take up all the interview time by showing off your extensive knowledge of the answer to the first one.

7) Be attentive

You only have 20 minutes or so, and you should keep your attention at its sharpest throughout. When a member is addressing a problem or question to you, give him your undivided attention. Address your reply principally to him, but do not exclude the other board members.

8) Do not interrupt

A board member may be stating a problem for you to analyze. He will ask you a question when the time comes. Let him state the problem, and wait for the question.

9) Make sure you understand the question

Do not try to answer until you are sure what the question is. If it is not clear, restate it in your own words or ask the board member to clarify it for you. However, do not haggle about minor elements.

10) Reply promptly but not hastily

A common entry on oral board rating sheets is "candidate responded readily," or "candidate hesitated in replies." Respond as promptly and quickly as you can, but do not jump to a hasty, ill-considered answer.

11) Do not be peremptory in your answers

A brief answer is proper – but do not fire your answer back. That is a losing game from your point of view. The board member can probably ask questions much faster than you can answer them.

12) Do not try to create the answer you think the board member wants

He is interested in what kind of mind you have and how it works – not in playing games. Furthermore, he can usually spot this practice and will actually grade you down on it.

13) Do not switch sides in your reply merely to agree with a board member

Frequently, a member will take a contrary position merely to draw you out and to see if you are willing and able to defend your point of view. Do not start a debate, yet do not surrender a good position. If a position is worth taking, it is worth defending.

14) Do not be afraid to admit an error in judgment if you are shown to be wrong

The board knows that you are forced to reply without any opportunity for careful consideration. Your answer may be demonstrably wrong. If so, admit it and get on with the interview.

15) Do not dwell at length on your present job

The opening question may relate to your present assignment. Answer the question but do not go into an extended discussion. You are being examined for a *new* job, not your present one. As a matter of fact, try to phrase ALL your answers in terms of the job for which you are being examined.

Basis of Rating

Probably you will forget most of these "do's" and "don'ts" when you walk into the oral interview room. Even remembering them all will not ensure you a passing grade. Perhaps you did not have the qualifications in the first place. But remembering them will help you to put your best foot forward, without treading on the toes of the board members.

Rumor and popular opinion to the contrary notwithstanding, an oral board wants you to make the best appearance possible. They know you are under pressure – but they also want to see how you respond to it as a guide to what your reaction would be under the pressures of the job you seek. They will be influenced by the degree of poise you display, the personal traits you show and the manner in which you respond.

ABOUT THIS BOOK

This book contains tests divided into Examination Sections. Go through each test, answering every question in the margin. We have also attached a sample answer sheet at the back of the book that can be removed and used. At the end of each test look at the answer key and check your answers. On the ones you got wrong, look at the right answer choice and learn. Do not fill in the answers first. Do not memorize the questions and answers, but understand the answer and principles involved. On your test, the questions will likely be different from the samples. Questions are changed and new ones added. If you understand these past questions you should have success with any changes that arise. Tests may consist of several types of questions. We have additional books on each subject should more study be advisable or necessary for you. Finally, the more you study, the better prepared you will be. This book is intended to be the last thing you study before you walk into the examination room. Prior study of relevant texts is also recommended. NLC publishes some of these in our Fundamental Series. Knowledge and good sense are important factors in passing your exam. Good luck also helps. So now study this Passbook, absorb the material contained within and take that knowledge into the examination. Then do your best to pass that exam.

EXAMINATION SECTION

EXAMINATION SECTION
TEST 1

DIRECTIONS: Each question or incomplete statement is followed by several suggested answers or completions. Select the one that BEST answers the question or completes the statement. *PRINT THE LETTER OF THE CORRECT ANSWER IN THE SPACE AT THE RIGHT.*

1. The cathode of a phototube is USUALLY coated with a thin layer of _____ oxide. 1.____

   A. magnesium   B. cesium   C. titanium   D. zinc

2. The capacitor on a capacitor motor is connected in _____ winding. 2.____

   A. parallel with the starting
   B. series with the running
   C. parallel with the running
   D. series with the starting

3. The refrigerant used in MOST modern home electric cooling appliances is 3.____

   A. neon   B. argon   C. zenon   D. freon

4. Splicing compound is USUALLY referred to as 4.____

   A. cable varnish   B. friction tape
   C. rubber tape   D. varnish cambric

5. The filament supports of an incandescent lamp are affixed to the 5.____

   A. button rod   B. lead-in wires
   C. steam seal   D. ceramic insulator

6. A non-tamperable fuse is known as a 6.____

   A. fusetron   B. fusetat
   C. circuit breaker   D. Kirkman tamp-lock

7. The wall plate used to cover two toggle switches mounted side by side in a wall box is known as a _____ plate. 7.____

   A. multiple toggle   B. duplex
   C. two gang   D. double

8. Building wire with a thermoplastic insulation is called type 8.____

   A. T.P.   B. R.H.   C. T.W.   D. RH-RW

9. A repulsion-start induction motor operates on 9.____

   A. 4 wire A.C.   B. single phase A.C.
   C. D.C. - 110V-220V   D. A.C. - D.C.

10. A *fish tape* is used to 10.____

    A. pull wires through a conduit   B. weatherproof a splice
    C. test a grounded circuit   D. support long cable runs

11. The color code of a 3 wire #12 cable is

    A. white black green B. blue black red
    C. white black red   D. red white green

12. The motor that has no brushes or commutator is known as a _____ motor.

    A. split phase   B. capacitor
    C. compound   D. shunt

13. The temperature of a well-designed continuously run motor, delivering its full rated horsepower, should NOT increase by more than _____ Fahrenheit.

    A. 40°   B. 52°   C. 60°   D. 72°

14. A floodlight operating at a point 500 feet from the meter, wired with #14 wire whose resistance is 2.575 ohms per 1000', has a voltage drop of *approximately* _____ volts.

    A. 5.7   B. 11.33   C. 12.74   D. 15.37

15. The grid in the vacuum tube was introduced by

    A. Fauere   B. Oersted   C. De Forest   D. Le Lanche

16. In an element for an electric range, the material that insulates the wire from the tube is

    A. magnesium oxide
    B. asbestos
    C. high temperature fibre glass
    D. titanium oxide

17. Most thermostats and relays that are used to activate and control a home heating system operate on _____ volts.

    A. 6   B. 24   C. 32   D. 46

18. The revolutions per minute of an electric motor can be determined by using a(n)

    A. hydrometer   B. tachometer
    C. pulse indicator D. prony brake

19. A record player pick-up arm, equipped with a phono cartridge that contains Rochelle-Salts, will produce a voltage known as

    A. phono-electric   B. bio-electric
    C. piezoelectric   D. pyrometric

20. The device that controls the flow of electrons in a solid is the

    A. electron tube   B. transistor
    C. anode   D. cathode

21. Fluorescent lamps are designed to operate on

    A. the rated voltage that appears on the lamp
    B. a rectifier controlled voltage
    C. a 115 volt or 230 volt circuit
    D. a circuit where the voltage fluctuation does not exceed 5%

22. The efficiency of a 3 horsepower motor that requires 2.4 kilowatts to drive it is   22._____

    A. 74%   B. 82%   C. 90%   D. 94%

23. The magnetic resistance that opposes the flow of magnetic current is   23._____

    A. inductance   B. reluctance
    C. reactance   D. impedance

24. The output in lumens per watt for an incandescent lamp (filament type) is _____ to _____ lumens.   24._____

    A. 14; 23   B. 30; 55   C. 50; 57   D. 58; 75

25. The voltage of a battery cell depends upon   25._____

    A. the number of lines cut per second
    B. the size of the plates and the distance they are set apart
    C. material that the plate is made of and the electrolyte used
    D. area of the zinc container

26. Most window-type air conditioners, such as used in the home, are equipped with a(n) _____ motor.   26._____

    A. synchronous   B. R-I
    C. seal-vac   D. hermetically sealed

27. Light that contains only a single color and also a single wave length is known as the _____ light.   27._____

    A. spectrum   B. laser
    C. aurora   D. sodium vapor

28. The *Edison effect* led to the development of the   28._____

    A. mercury vapor lamp   B. radio tube
    C. phonograph   D. fluorescent lamp

29. A device for producing high tension induced current is the _____ coil.   29._____

    A. Ruhmkorff   B. Solenoid   C. Thury   D. Choke

30. In a triode tube, the element placed between the cathode and the plate is called   30._____

    A. rectifier   B. controlled grid
    C. S C C   D. D C C

KEY (CORRECT ANSWERS)

1.	B	11.	C	21.	C
2.	D	12.	A	22.	D
3.	D	13.	D	23.	B
4.	C	14.	C	24.	A
5.	A	15.	C	25.	C
6.	B	16.	A	26.	D
7.	C	17.	B	27.	B
8.	C	18.	B	28.	B
9.	B	19.	C	29.	A
10.	A	20.	B	30.	B

TEST 2

DIRECTIONS: Each question or incomplete statement is followed by several suggested answers or completions. Select the one that BEST answers the question or completes the statement. *PRINT THE LETTER OF THE CORRECT ANSWER IN THE SPACE AT THE RIGHT.*

1. A fixture hickey is used to

    A. bend pipe
    B. suspend a ceiling light
    C. make a 60° offset in BX
    D. ground a fixture

2. Nichrome wire is used in electrical heating devices because it

    A. is non-magnetic
    B. has a low melting point
    C. is cheaper than copper wire
    D. has a high resistance

3. The letters *E M T* in conduit work refer to

    A. underwriters approval
    B. thin wall conduit
    C. A.C. use only
    D. ready for first inspection

4. A 120 volt three-way incandescent lamp bulb has

    A. one filament
    B. two filaments
    C. three filaments
    D. a variable resistor

5. When an object to be copperplated is immersed in its electrolyte, it should be connected to the

    A. anode
    B. cathode
    C. right terminal
    D. electrolyte

6. A voltmeter consists of a milliammeter and a high resistance which are connected in

    A. multiple   B. parallel   C. series   D. shunt

7. A device for producing electricity directly from heat is called a

    A. turbine
    B. thermocouple
    C. transformer
    D. rheostat

8. The combined resistance of a circuit containing five 40 ohm resistances in parallel is _____ ohms.

    A. 8   B. 20   C. 40   D. 200

9. An alternator differs from a D.C. generator because it has no

    A. brushes
    B. commutator
    C. field poles
    D. rotor

10. The resistance of a wire 1/16 inch in diameter is one OHM. A wire of the same length, but twice the diameter, has a resistance of ohms.

    A. 1/4   B. 1/2   C. 1   D. 2

11. A device that measures energy consumption of electricity is called a   11._____
    A. wattmeter   B. kilowatthourmeter
    C. kilowatt meter   D. ammeter

12. A *universal* motor is a(n) _____ motor.   12._____
    A. shunt   B. induction   C. series   D. synchronous

13. In a three phase, four wire, 208 volt distribution system, the voltage between any phase   13._____
    wire and the neutral is _____ volts.
    A. 0   B. 120   C. 208   D. 240

14. Of the following, the motor that does NOT have a commutator is   14._____
    A. universal   B. series
    C. repulsion induction   D. split phase

15. An incandescent lamp rated at 130 volts-100 watts, and operated at 115 volts will   15._____
    A. consume more wattage and impair the life of the filament
    B. increase lamp life and reduce wattage consumed
    C. produce fewer lumens per watt and increase lamp efficiency
    D. have no effect on the lamp

16. A 2 horsepower 75% efficient D.C. motor operating at full load draws *approximately*   16._____
    _____ watts.
    A. 1000   B. 1500   C. 2000   D. 3000

17. An insulating material that withstands heat better than wire with more ordinary insulation   17._____
    is
    A. rubber   B. plastic
    C. rubber with cotton covering D. varnished cambric

18. Electrical resistance can be measured with a(n)   18._____
    A. voltmeter and an ammeter   B. A.C. wattmeter
    C. thermocouple   D. induction coil

19. The property of a circuit that enables it to store electrical energy in the form of an electro-   19._____
    static field is called
    A. inductance   B. reactance
    C. resistance   D. capacitance

20. If a 50 ohm resistance draws two amperes from a circuit, the power it uses is   20._____
    A. 0.2 KW   B. 25 watts
    C. 100 watts   D. none of the above

21. The world's FIRST central light and power plant was developed by
    A. Samuel F.B. Morse
    B. Lee De Forest
    C. Edwin H. Armstrong
    D. Thomas A. Edison

22. A *tuner* circuit consists of a
    A. zener diode and tunnel transistor
    B. capacitor and inductance coil
    C. resistor and R.F. amplifier tube
    D. resistor and capacitor

23. A hotplate having a resistance of 30 ohms, connected to a 120 volt outlet, would draw a current of _____ amperes.
    A. 4   B. 90   C. 150   D. 3600

24. Of the following, the term that does NOT relate to magnetism is
    A. reluctance
    B. oersted
    C. coulomb
    D. magneto-motive force

25. A basic difference between radio waves and sound waves is that radio waves are
    A. of a different frequency
    B. electrical currents
    C. molecules of air in motion
    D. electromagnetic waves

26. An object that has a positive electrostatic charge would have an excess of
    A. electrons
    B. protons
    C. neutrons
    D. omega minus particles

27. Of the following, the statement that does NOT apply to a capacitor is that it can
    A. store electrons
    B. pass alternating current
    C. pass direct current
    D. be used to smooth out pulsating direct current

28. The section of a radio transmitter or receiver that causes a stream of electrons to vibrate back and forth at high frequencies is known as a(n)
    A. modulator   B. oscillator   C. amplifier   D. detector

29. The separation of speech or music from a radio wave carrying music or speech is referred to as
    A. audio filtration
    B. separation
    C. demodulation
    D. tracing

30. A circuit used to smooth out the surges of pulsating direct current from a rectifier is called a
    A. filter
    B. multiplexer
    C. demodulator
    D. local oscillator

KEY (CORRECT ANSWERS)

1. B	11. B	21. D
2. D	12. C	22. B
3. B	13. B	23. A
4. B	14. D	24. C
5. B	15. B	25. D
6. C	16. C	26. B
7. B	17. D	27. C
8. A	18. A	28. B
9. B	19. D	29. C
10. A	20. A	30. A

TEST 3

DIRECTIONS: Each question or incomplete statement is followed by several suggested answers or completions. Select the one that BEST answers the question or completes the statement. *PRINT THE LETTER OF THE CORRECT ANSWER IN THE SPACE AT THE RIGHT.*

1. The simple motor found in an electric clock is called a(n) _____ motor.   1.____

    A. synchronous B. induction
    C. rotor D. D.C.

2. The amperage of a fully charged car storage battery is USUALLY near _____ amps.   2.____

    A. 10 B. 100 C. 1000 D. 10,000

3. To prevent the initial surge of current drawn by an electric motor from *burning out* the fuse in the circuit, one uses a   3.____

    A. cartridge fuse B. circuit breaker
    C. plug fuse D. fusetron

4. The many radio waves striking the antenna of a receiver are tuned-in with the   4.____

    A. transformer B. choke coil
    C. variable condenser D. diode detector

5. The starting motor of an automobile engine is shifted into mesh with the flywheel gear by a   5.____

    A. vibrator B. solenoid
    C. bendix D. starter button

6. The picture tube of a television set is also referred to as a _____ tube.   6.____

    A. cathode-ray B. power beam
    C. oscilliscope D. photo-electric

7. Generators that have two or more sets of field poles and require fewer revolutions to generate a 60-cycle-per second current are called   7.____

    A. duo-dynamos B. vibrators
    C. poly-phase generators D. alternators

8. A bar that has been artificially magnetized can be demagnetized by   8.____

    A. quenching it in hot oil
    B. pounding it with a heavy hammer
    C. bending it into a *U* shape
    D. wrapping it in insulating tape

9. The part of a generator which determines if it is a direct current generator is the   9.____

    A. stator B. field C. commutator D. brush

10. The term which refers to pressure or force in electric current is   10.____

    A. amperage B. voltage C. ohms D. electrons

9

11. Nichrome wire is MOST likely to be found in a(n)

    A. T.V. circuit B. electric motor
    C. electric clock D. electric heater

12. Electromagnetic waves are changed into pulses capable of producing sound waves in a radio by means of a

    A. transformer B. speaker
    C. detector D. oscillator

13. The SIMPLEST form of electronic tube is called

    A. cathode B. diode C. plate D. triode

14. Of the following, the one that is NOT a part of a radio tube is the

    A. envelope B. plate C. condenser D. filament

15. The speed of a simple electric motor can be controlled with the use of a

    A. variable resistor B. electrolytic condenser
    C. variable condenser D. prony-brake

16. A single wet cell can be made from a copper penny and a *zinc* penny attached to two copper leads immersed in

    A. mineral oil B. salt-water solution
    C. distilled water D. chromate of soda

17. The MINIMUM gauge wire for house circuits should be

    A. 10 B. 18 C. 14 D. 22

18. The safety device used in a house wiring circuit to protect against an overload is a

    A. circuit breaker B. knife switch
    C. cut-off D. mercury switch

19. To prevent the generator from burning out at high speeds, the battery circuit of the automobile employs a

    A. choke coil B. variable resistor
    C. voltage regulator D. current trap

20. An interrupted current of 6 volts flows in the primary circuit of an induction coil of 100 turns of wire. If the secondary coil has 1,000 turns, the theoretical voltage output is

    A. .6 B. 60 C. 600 D. .06

21. A 200 watt bulb in a 100 volt circuit uses _____ ampere(s).

    A. .2 B. .02 C. 2 D. 20

22. A 220 volt air conditioner drawing 15 amperes of current operates 10 hours a day. The total cost of operation for four weeks at the rate of 4 cents per kilowatt hour would be

    A. $18.48 B. $55.44 C. $26.40 D. $36.96

23. If a dry cell battery is capable of supplying a force of two volts and ten amperes of current, connecting five such batteries in parallel will result in a total capacity of _____ volts with _____ amperes.

    A. 2; 50 B. 20; 10 C. 10; 50 D. 10; 10

24. To calculate the number of turns of wire needed to make a step-up or step-down transformer when the voltages are known, and one set of windings is determined, we use the following formula:

    A. $\dfrac{\text{Primary turns}}{\text{Secondary turns}} = \dfrac{\text{Primary volts}}{\text{Secondary volts}}$

    B. $\dfrac{\text{Primary turns}}{\text{Primary volts}} = \dfrac{\text{Secondary volts}}{\text{Secondary turns}}$

    C. $\dfrac{\text{Primary turns}}{\text{Secondary volts}} = \dfrac{\text{Primary volts}}{\text{Secondary turns}}$

    D. $\dfrac{\text{Primary turns}}{\text{Secondary volts}} = \dfrac{\text{Primary volts}}{\text{Secondary turns}}$

25. To measure the specific gravity of the contents of a storage battery, one uses a

    A. hygrometer B. galvanometer
    C. ammeter   D. hydrometer

26. Lightning is _____ electricity.

    A. induced B. ionized C. static D. magnetic

27. A lodestone is related to

    A. magnetism   B. resistance
    C. conductivity D. reluctance

28. The term related to a storer of electricity is

    A. milliampere B. microfarad
    C. megohm   D. microvolt

29. The thermostat as a switch employs the use of a

    A. diode tube   B. tungsten filament
    C. bimetallic strip D. thermocouple

30. In servicing electrical apparatus, it is necessary to know the values of amperage, voltage, and resistance. When two of the factors are known, the third may be found by applying *Ohm's Law*.
    Of the following formulas, the one that does NOT apply is

    A. I = R/I B. R = E/I C. E = IR D. I = E/R

KEY (CORRECT ANSWERS)

1.	A	11.	D	21.	C
2.	B	12.	C	22.	D
3.	D	13.	B	23.	A
4.	C	14.	C	24.	A
5.	B	15.	A	25.	D
6.	A	16.	B	26.	C
7.	D	17.	C	27.	A
8.	B	18.	A	28.	B
9.	C	19.	C	29.	C
10.	B	20.	B	30.	A

TEST 4

DIRECTIONS: Each question or incomplete statement is followed by several suggested answers or completions. Select the one that BEST answers the question or completes the statement. *PRINT THE LETTER OF THE CORRECT ANSWER IN THE SPACE AT THE RIGHT.*

1. The effect of a capacitor on direct current is to _____ it.

    A. modulate
    B. block
    C. pass
    D. demodulate

    1._____

2. Factors which determine the resistance of a wire are:

    A. Diameter, insulating material, length, strands
    B. Length, diameter, material, temperature
    C. Material, light factor, pressure, circumference
    D. Pressure, magnetism, binding, length

    2._____

3. Current flow in a triode vacuum tube may be controlled by the

    A. plate and the grid
    B. filament and the plate
    C. grid and the heater
    D. cathode and the filament

    3._____

4. If the resistance in a parallel circuit is *increased*, the voltage drop across a resistor would

    A. *increase*
    B. vary proportionally
    C. *decrease*
    D. remain the same

    4._____

5. In parallel and series circuits, current is

    A. inversely proportional to resistance and directly proportional to voltage
    B. directly proportional to resistance and inversely proportional to voltage
    C. not affected by voltage
    D. not affected by resistance

    5._____

6. The process of mixing audio waves with radio waves is called

    A. rectification
    B. attenuation
    C. modulation
    D. superimposition

    6._____

7. Transistors are made of three parts: a base, a collector, and an emitter. When compared to a vacuum tube, the collector is comparable to the

    A. grid   B. plate   C. cathode   D. filament

    7._____

8. Resistance wire used in electrical appliances is *usually* an alloy of

    A. tungsten, chromium, brass
    B. nickel, chromium, iron
    C. copper, nickel, tungsten
    D. iron, copper, molybdenum

    8._____

9. A meter with terminals connected in series and across the line is a

    A. voltmeter   B. ammeter   C. ohmmeter   D. wattmeter

    9._____

10. One hundred volts will push _____ milliamperes through 20k ohms of resistance.

    A. 2   B. 5   C. 50   D. 2000

    10._____

11. A resistor having bands of orange, red, yellow, and silver would have a resistance value of _____ ohms.

    A. 32k B. 320k C. 2.3 meg D. 43 meg

12. A flashbulb used for photographic purposes contains

    A. aluminum and oxygen
    B. tungsten and helium
    C. aluminum and hydrogen
    D. tungsten and argon

13. A generator having a cummutator produces _____ current.

    A. alternating
    B. direct
    C. synchronous
    D. modulating

14. A step-down transformer has 1,200 turns on the primary. 90 volts is applied to the primary, and the second is to produce 15 volts.
    How many turns should be wound on the secondary?

    A. 200 B. 600 C. 7,200 D. 108,000

15. In a radio circuit, a transformer CANNOT be used to

    A. step-up a-c voltage
    B. isolate part of a circuit
    C. step-down d-c voltage
    D. couple part of a circuit to another

16. A transformer has 200 turns of #14 wire wound on primary and 1,000 turns of #14 wire wound on the secondary.
    A voltmeter attached to the secondary terminals would indicate _____ volts if 50 volts were attached to the
    primary.

    A. 0 B. 10 C. 250 D. 600

17. Service entrance cable for the typical home is usually made up of three wires.
    The *hot* wires are usually No.

    A. 4 or No. 6
    B. 8 or No. 10
    C. 12 or No. 14
    D. 16 or No. 18

18. In the PNP type transistor, the collector is *normally*

    A. negative
    B. positive
    C. shorted out
    D. not needed

19. In a beam power tube, the screen grid is

    A. the plate
    B. positive
    C. the suppressor
    D. negative

20. A silicon controlled rectifier is

    A. a nuvistor
    B. a CRT
    C. thermally operated
    D. a semi-conductor

21. In copper plating a metallic object, it should be placed at the

    A. anode   B. switch   C. cathode   D. electrolyte

22. At five cents per kilowatt hour, a 100-watt lamp which is operated for one hundred (100) hours would use energy that would cost

    A. 5 cents   B. less than 10 cents
    C. 50 cents   D. 5 dollars

23. A galvanometer may be converted to a voltmeter by adding a

    A. shunt in series   B. multiplier in series
    C. multiplier in parallel D. shunt in parallel

24. The counter emf of an inductance coil is measured in

    A. milliamperes   B. microfarads
    C. henrys   D. millivolts

25. A fluorescent lamp lights when the

    A. ballast coil produces a high-voltage charge
    B. starter switch is placed in parallel with the filament
    C. mercury forms minute droplets on the filament
    D. ballast changes the A.C. to D.C. in the tube

26. The electrolyte used in a dry cell is composed of

    A. carbon, magnesium oxide, ammonia, sodium chloride
    B. sodium, manganese dioxide, alumina, zinc sulphate
    C. carbon, manganese dioxide, sal ammoniac, zinc chloride
    D. sodium, magnesium sulphate, arsenic, zinc oxide

27. A variable capacitor has its capacitance *increased* when the

    A. plates are open
    B. rotor is attached to the stator
    C. plates are meshed
    D. dielectric is given a full charge

28. The gas mixture commonly used in incandescent lamps is

    A. nitrogen and argon   B. nitrogen and helium
    C. helium and argon   D. hydrogen and oxygen

29. A motor with a high-starting torque and rapid acceleration is a(n) _____ motor.

    A. D.C. shunt wound   B. D.C. series wound
    C. A.C. synchronous   D. A.C. split phase

30. Bry cells used for powering cordless electric razors are usually _____ cells.

    A. manganese alkaline   B. nickel cadmium
    C. nickel silver   D. zinc carbon

KEY (CORRECT ANSWERS)

1.	B	11.	B	21.	C
2.	B	12.	A	22.	C
3.	A	13.	B	23.	B
4.	D	14.	A	24.	C
5.	A	15.	C	25.	A
6.	C	16.	A	26.	C
7.	B	17.	A	27.	C
8.	B	18.	A	28.	A
9.	D	19.	B	29.	B
10.	B	20.	D	30.	B

EXAMINATION SECTION
TEST 1

DIRECTIONS: Each question or incomplete statement is followed by several suggested answers or completions. Select the one that BEST answers the question or completes the statement. *PRINT THE LETTER OF THE CORRECT ANSWER IN THE SPACE AT THE RIGHT.*

Questions 1-6.

DIRECTIONS: Questions 1 through 6 are to be answered on the basis of the circuit diagram below. All switches are initially open.

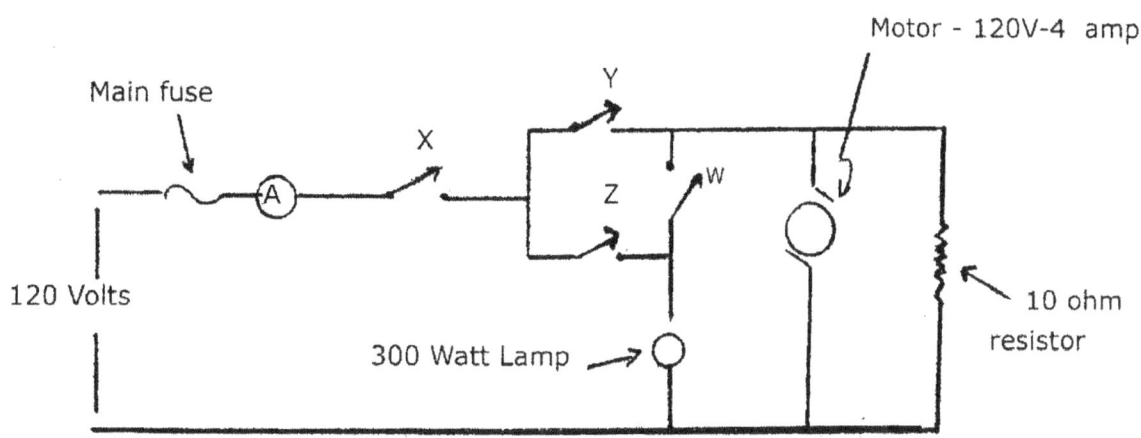

1. To light the 300 watt lamp, the following switches MUST be closed: 1.____

   A. X and Y   B. Y and Z   C. X and Z   D. X and W

2. If all of the switches W, X, Y, and Z are closed, the following will happen: 2.____

   A. The lamp will light and the motor will rotate
   B. The lamp will light and the motor will not rotate
   C. The lamp will not light and the motor will not rotate
   D. A short circuit will occur and the main fuse will blow

3. With 120 volts applied across the 10 ohm resistor, the current drawn by the resistor is _____ amp(s). 3.____

   A. 1/12   B. 1.2   C. 12   D. 1200

4. With 120 volts applied to the 10 ohm resistor, the power used by the resistor is _____ kw. 4.____

   A. 1.44   B. 1.2   C. .144   D. .12

5. The current drawn by the 300 watt lamp when lighted should be APPROXIMATELY _____ amps. 5.____

   A. 2.5   B. 3.6   C. 25   D. 36

6. In the circuit shown, the symbol A is used to indicate a (n)   6._____

   A. ammeter   B. *and* circuit
   C. voltmeter   D. wattmeter

7. Of the following materials, the BEST conductor of electricity is   7._____

   A. iron   B. copper   C. aluminum   D. glass

8. The sum of 6'6", 5'9", and 2' 1 1/2" is   8._____

   A. 13'4 1/2"   B. 13'6 1/2"   C. 14'4 1/2"   D. 14'6 1/2"

9.   9._____

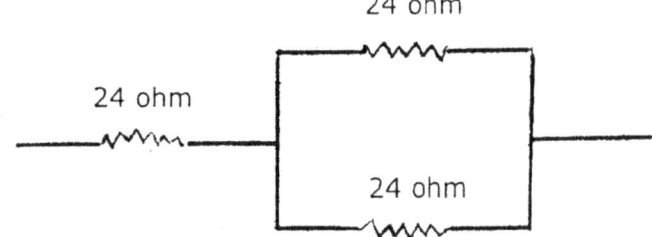

   The equivalent resistance of the three resistors shown in the sketch above is _____ ohms.

   A. 8   B. 24   C. 36   D. 72

10.   10._____

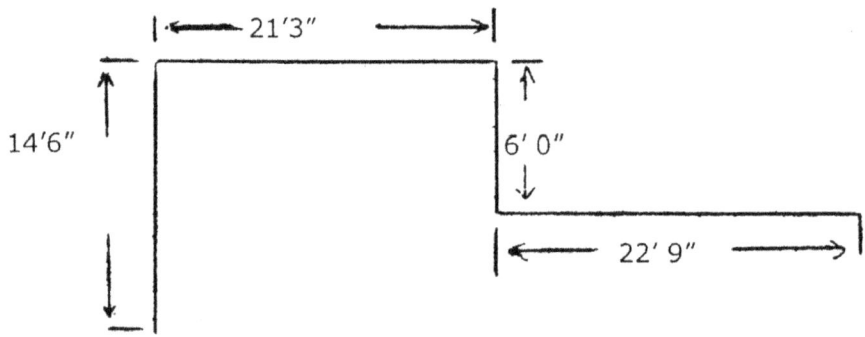

   The TOTAL length of electrical conduit that must be run along the path shown on the diagram above is

   A. 63'8"   B. 64'6"   C. 65'6"   D. 66'8"

11. Of the following electrical devices, the one that is NOT normally used in direct current electrical circuits is a (n)   11._____

   A. circuit breaker   B. double-pole switch
   C. transformer   D. inverter

12. The number of 120-volt light bulbs that should NORMALLY be connected in series across a 600-volt electric line is   12._____

   A. 1   B. 2   C. 3   D. 5

13. Of the following motors, the one that does NOT have any brushes is the _____ motor.   13._____

    A. d.c. shunt   B. d.c. series
    C. squirrel cage induction   D. compound

14. Of the following materials, the one that is COMMONLY used as an electric heating element in an electric heater is   14._____

    A. zinc   B. brass
    C. terne plate   D. nichrome

Questions 15-25.

DIRECTIONS: Questions 15 through 25 are to be answered on the basis of the instruments listed below. Each instrument is listed with an identifying number in front of it.

    1 - Hygrometer   9 - Vernier caliper
    2 - Ammeter   10 - Wire gage
    3 - Voltmeter   11 - 6-foot folding rule
    4 - Wattmeter   12 - Architect's scale
    5 - Megger   13 - Planimeter
    6 - Oscilloscope   14 - Engineer's scale
    7 - Frequency meter   15 - Ohmmeter
    8 - Micrometer

15. The instrument that should be used to accurately measure the resistance of a 4,700 ohm resistor is Number   15._____

    A. 3   B. 4   C. 7   D. 15

16. To measure the current in an electrical circuit, the instrument that should be used is Number   16._____

    A. 2   B. 7   C. 8   D. 15

17. To measure the insulation resistance of a rubber-covered electrical cable, the instrument that should be used is Number   17._____

    A. 4   B. 5   C. 8   D. 15

18. An AC motor is hooked up to a power distribution box.
    In order to check the voltage at the motor terminals, the instrument that should be used is Number   18._____

    A. 2   B. 3   C. 4   D. 7

19. To measure the shaft diameter of a motor accurately to one-thousandth of an inch, the instrument that should be used is Number   19._____

    A. 8   B. 10   C. 11   D. 14

20. The instrument that should be used to determine whether 25 Hz. or 60 Hz. is present in an electrical circuit is Number   20._____

    A. 4   B. 5   C. 7   D. 8

21. Of the following, the PROPER instrument to use to determine the diameter of the conductor of a piece of electrical hook-up wire is Number

    A. 10   B. 11   C. 12   D. 14

22. The amount of electrical power being used in a balanced three-phase circuit should be measured with Number

    A. 2   B. 3   C. 4   D. 5

23. The electrical wave form at a given point in an electronic circuit can be observed with Number

    A. 2   B. 3   C. 6   D. 7

24. The PROPER instrument to use for measuring the width of a door is Number

    A. 11   B. 12   C. 13   D. 14

25. A one-inch hole with a tolerance of plus or minus three-thousandths is reamed in a steel block.
    The PROPER instrument to use to accurately check the diameter of the hole is Number

    A. 8   B. 9   C. 11   D. 14

KEY (CORRECT ANSWERS)

1. C
2. A
3. C
4. A
5. A
6. A
7. B
8. C
9. C
10. B
11. C
12. D
13. C
14. D
15. D
16. A
17. B
18. B
19. A
20. C
21. A
22. C
23. C
24. A
25. B

TEST 2

DIRECTIONS: Each question or incomplete statement is followed by several suggested answers or completions. Select the one that BEST answers the question or completes the statement. *PRINT THE LETTER OF THE CORRECT ANSWER IN THE SPACE AT THE RIGHT.*

1. The number of conductors required to connect a 3-phase delta connected heater bank to an electric power panel board is 1.____

    A. 2 B. 3 C. 4 D. 5

2. Of the following, the wire size that is MOST commonly used for branch lighting circuits in homes is _____ A.W.G. 2.____

    A. #12 B. #8 C. #6 D. #4

3. When installing electrical circuits, the tool that should be used to pull wire through a conduit is a 3.____

    A. mandrel B. snake
    C. rod D. pulling iron

4. Of the following AC voltages, the LOWEST voltage that a neon test lamp can detect is _____ volts. 4.____

    A. 6 B. 12 C. 80 D. 120

5. Of the following, the BEST procedure to use when storing tools that are subject to rusting is to 5.____

    A. apply a thin coating of soap onto the tools
    B. apply a light coating of oil to the tools
    C. wrap the tools in clean cheesecloth
    D. place the tools in a covered container

6. If a 3 1/2 inch long nail is required to nail wood framing members together, the nail size to use should be 6.____

    A. 2d B. 4d C. 16d D. 60d

7. Of the four motors listed below, the one that can operate only on alternating current is a(n) _____ motor. 7.____

    A. series B. shunt
    C. compound D. induction

8. The sum of 1/3 + 2/5 + 5/6 is 8.____

    A. 1 17/30 B. 1 3/5 C. 1 15/24 D. 1 5/6

9. Of the following instruments, the one that should be used to measure the state of charge of a lead-acid storage battery is a(n) 9.____

    A. ammeter B. ohmmeter
    C. hydrometer D. thermometer

21

10. If three 1 1/2 volt dry cell batteries are wired in series, the TOTAL voltage provided by the three batteries is _____ volts.

    A. 1.5   B. 3   C. 4.5   D. 6.0

11. Taking into account time and one-half payment for time over 40 hours of work, the gross pay of an employee who works 43 hours in a week at a rate of pay of $10.68 per hour is

    A. $427.20   B. $459.24   C. $475.26   D. $491.28

12. The sum of 0.365 + 3.941 + 10.676 + 0.784 is

    A. 13.766   B. 15.666   C. 15.756   D. 15.766

13. In order to transmit mechanical power between two rotating shafts at right angles to each other, two gears are used. Of the following, the type of gears that should be used are _____ gears.

    A. herringbone   B. spur
    C. bevel   D. rack and pinion

14. To properly ground the service electrical equipment in a building, a ground connection should be made to _____ the building.

    A. the waste or soil line leaving
    B. the vent line going to the exterior of
    C. any steel beam in
    D. the cold water line entering

15. The area of the triangle shown at the right is _____ square inches.
    A. 120
    B. 240
    C. 360
    D. 480

Questions 16-25.

DIRECTIONS: Questions 16 through 25 are to be answered on the basis of the tools shown on the next page. The tools are not shown to scale. Each tool is shown with an identifying number alongside it.

3 (#2)

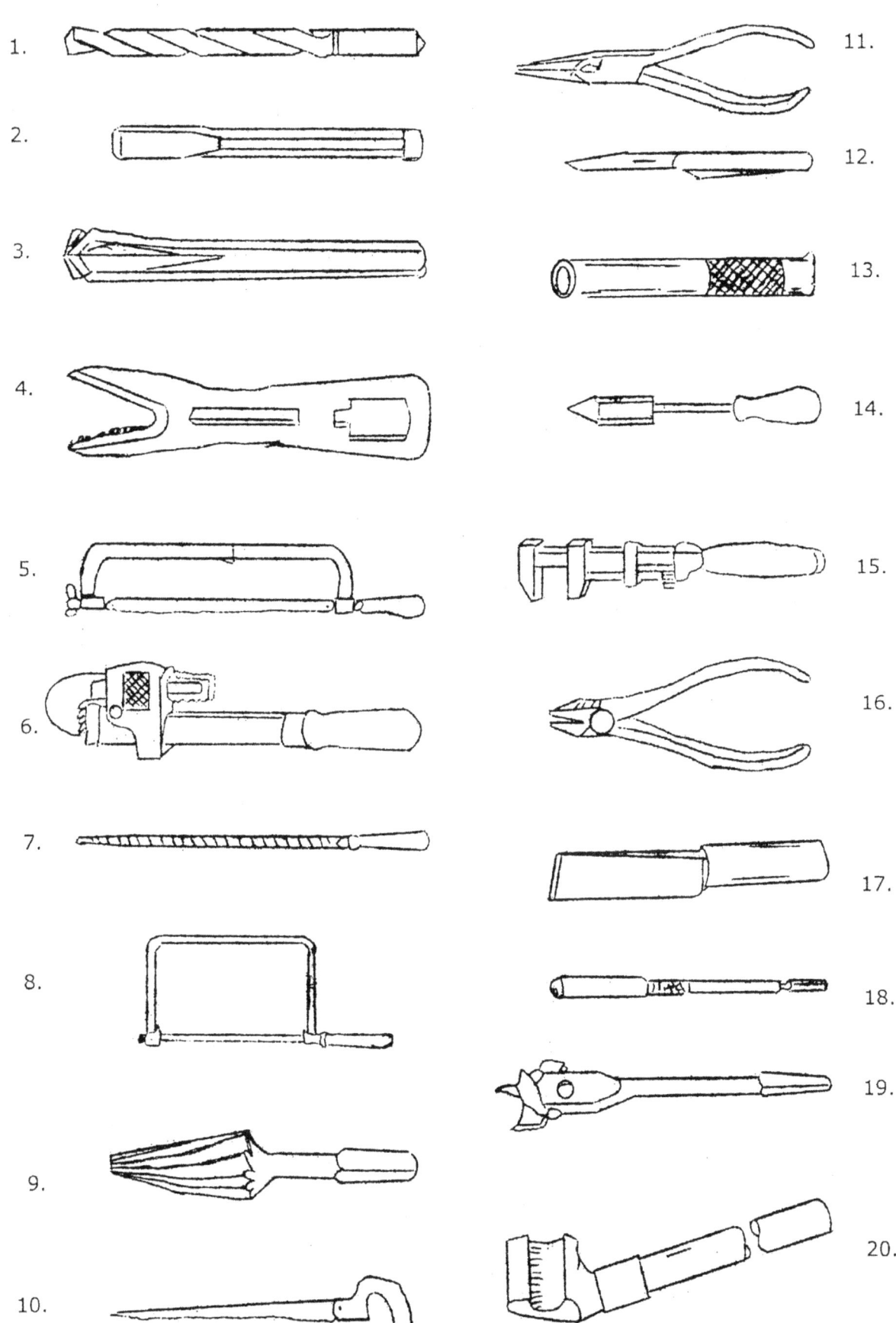

1.
2.
3.
4.
5.
6.
7.
8.
9.
10.
11.
12.
13.
14.
15.
16.
17.
18.
19.
20.

16. The tool that should be used for cutting thin wall steel conduit is Number   16._____
    A. 5   B. 8   C. 10   D. 16

17. The tool that should be used for cutting a 1 7/8 inch diameter hole in a wood joist is Number   17._____
    A. 3   B. 9   C. 14   D. 19

18. The tool that should be used for soldering splices in electrical wire is Number   18._____
    A. 3   B. 7   C. 13   D. 14

19. After cutting off a piece of 3/4 inch diameter electrical conduit, the tool that should be   19._____
    used for removing a burr from the inside of the conduit is Number
    A. 9   B. 11   C. 12   D. 14

20. The tool that should be used for turning a coupling onto a threaded conduit is Number   20._____
    A. 6   B. 11   C. 15   D. 16

21. The tool that should be used for cutting wood lathing in plaster walls is Number   21._____
    A. 5   B. 7   C. 10   D. 12

22. The tool that should be used for drilling a 3/8 inch diameter hole in a steel beam is Number   22._____
    A. 1   B. 2   C. 3   D. 9

23. Of the following, the BEST tool to use for stripping insulation from electrical hook-up wire   23._____
    is Number
    A. 11   B. 12   C. 15   D. 20

24. The tool that should be used for bending an electrical wire around a terminal post is   24._____
    Number
    A. 4   B. 11   C. 15   D. 16

25. The tool that should be used for cutting electrical hookup wire is Number   25._____
    A. 5   B. 12   C. 16   D. 17

KEY (CORRECT ANSWERS)

1.	B	11.	C
2.	A	12.	D
3.	B	13.	C
4.	C	14.	D
5.	B	15.	A
6.	C	16.	A
7.	D	17.	D
8.	A	18.	D
9.	C	19.	A
10.	C	20.	A

21. C
22. A
23. B
24. B
25. C

TEST 3

DIRECTIONS: Each question or incomplete statement is followed by several suggested answers or completions. Select the one that BEST answers the question or completes the statement. *PRINT THE LETTER OF THE CORRECT ANSWER IN THE SPACE AT THE RIGHT.*

1. An electric circuit has current flowing through it. The panel board switch feeding the circuit is opened, causing arcing across the switch contacts.
Generally, this arcing is caused by

    A. a lack of energy storage in the circuit
    B. electrical energy stored by a capacitor
    C. electrical energy stored by a resistor
    D. magnetic energy induced by an inductance

    1.____

2. MOST filter capacitors in radios have a capacity rating given in

    A. microvolts   B. milliamps
    C. millihenries   D. microfarads

    2.____

3. Of the following, the electrical wire size that is COMMONLY used for telephone circuits is _____ A.W.G.

    A. #6   B. #10   C. #12   D. #22

    3.____

Questions 4-9.

DIRECTIONS: Questions 4 through 9 are to be answered on the basis of the electrical circuit diagram shown below, where letters are used to identify various circuit components.

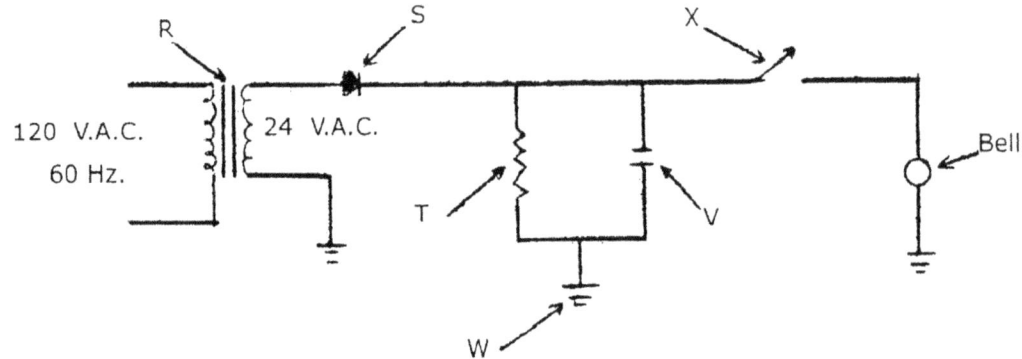

4. The device indicated by the letter R is a

    A. capacitor   B. converter
    C. resistor   D. transformer

    4.____

5. The device indicated by the letter S is a

    A. transistor   B. diode
    C. thermistor   D. directional relay

    5.____

2 (#3)

6. The devices indicated by the letters T and V are used together to _____ components of the secondary current. 6._____

   A. reduce the AC B. reduce the DC
   C. transform the AC D. invert the AC

7. The letter W points to a standard electrical symbol for a 7._____

   A. wire B. ground
   C. terminal D. lightning arrestor

8. Closing switch X will apply the following type of voltage to the bell: 8._____

   A. 60 Hz. AC B. DC
   C. pulsating AC D. 120 Hz. AC

9. The circuit shown contains a _____ rectifier. 9._____

   A. mercury-arc B. full-wave
   C. bridge D. half-wave

10. A bolt specified as 1/4-28 means the following: 10._____
    The

    A. bolt is 1/4 inch in diameter and has 28 threads per inch
    B. bolt is 1/4 inch in diameter and is 2.8 inches long
    C. bolt is 1/4 inch long and has 28 threads
    D. threaded portion of the bolt is 1/4 inch long and has 28 threads per inch

11. When cutting 0.045-inch thickness sheet metal, it is BEST to use a hacksaw blade that has _____ teeth per inch. 11._____

    A. 7 B. 12 C. 18 D. 32

12. To accurately tighten a bolt to 28 foot-pounds, it is BEST to use a(n) _____ wrench. 12._____

    A. pipe B. open end C. box D. torque

13. When bending a 2-inch diameter conduit, the CORRECT tool to use is a 13._____

    A. hickey B. pipe wrench
    C. hydraulic bender D. stock and die

14. When soldering two #20 A.W.G. copper wires together to form a splice, the solder that SHOULD be used is _____ solder. 14._____

    A. acid-core B. solid-core
    C. rosin-core D. liquid

15. A bathroom heating unit draws 10 amperes at 115 volts. 15._____
    The hot resistance of the heating unit should be _____ ohms.

    A. .08 B. 8 C. 11.5 D. 1150

16. Of the following materials, the one that is NOT suitable as an electrical insulator is 16._____

    A. glass B. mica C. rubber D. platinum

17. An air conditioning unit is rated at 1000 watts. The unit is run for 10 hours per day, five days per week.
If the cost for electrical energy is 5 cents per kilowatt-hour, the weekly cost for electricity should be

    A. 25¢   B. 50¢   C. $2.50   D. $25.00

18. If a fuse is protecting the circuit of a 15 ohm electric heater and it is designed to blow out at a current exceeding 10 amperes, the MAXIMUM voltage from among the following that should be applied across the terminals of the heater is _____ volts.

    A. 110   B. 120   C. 160   D. 600

19. Before opening a pneumatic hose connection, it is important to remove pressure from the hose line PRIMARILY to avoid

    A. losing air
    B. personal injury
    C. damage to the hose connection
    D. a build-up of pressure in the air compressor

20. If the scale on a shop drawing is 1/4 inch to the foot, then a part which measures 3 3/8 inches long on the drawing has an ACTUAL length of _____ feet _____ inches.

    A. 12; 6   B. 13; 6   C. 13; 9   D. 14; 9

21. The function that is USUALLY performed by a motor controller is to

    A. start and stop a motor
    B. protect a motor from a short circuit
    C. prevent bearing failure of a motor
    D. control the brush wear in a motor

22. Of the following galvanized sheet metal electrical outlet boxes, the one that is NOT a commonly used size is the _____ box.

    A. 4" square   B. 4" octagonal
    C. 4" x 2 1/8"   D. 4" x 1"

23. When soldering a transistor into a circuit, it is MOST important to protect the transistor from

    A. the application of an excess of rosin flux
    B. excessive heat
    C. the application of an excess of solder
    D. too much pressure

24. When installing BX type cable, it is important to protect the wires in the cable from the cut ends of the armored sheath.
The APPROVED method of providing this protection is to

    A. use a fiber or plastic insulating bushing
    B. file the cut ends of the sheath smooth
    C. use a connector where the cable enters a junction box
    D. tie the wires into an Underwriter's knot

25. While lifting a heavy piece of equipment off the floor, a person should NOT

   A. twist his body
   B. grasp it firmly
   C. maintain a solid footing on the ground
   D. bend his knees

26. It is important that metal cabinets and panels that house electrical equipment should be grounded PRIMARILY in order to

   A. prevent short circuits from occurring
   B. keep all circuits at ground potential
   C. minimize shock hazards
   D. reduce the effects of electrolytic corrosion

27. A foreman explains a technical procedure to a new employee. If the employee does not understand the instructions he has received, it would be BEST if he were to

   A. follow the procedure as best he could
   B. ask the foreman to explain it to him again
   C. avoid following the procedure
   D. ask the foreman to give him other work

28. Of the following, the BEST connectors to use when mounting an electrical panel box directly onto a concrete wall are

   A. threaded studs   B. machine screws
   C. lag screws   D. expansion bolts

29. Of the following, the BEST instrument to use to measure the small gap between relay contacts is

   A. a micrometer   B. a feeler gage
   C. inside calipers   D. a plug gage

30. A POSSIBLE result of mounting a 40 ampere fuse in a fuse box for a circuit requiring a 20 ampere fuse is that the 40 ampere fuse may

   A. provide twice as much protection to the circuit from overloads
   B. blow more easily than the smaller fuse due to an overload
   C. cause serious damage to the circuit from an overload
   D. reduce power consumption in the circuit

KEY (CORRECT ANSWERS)

1.	D	16.	D
2.	D	17.	C
3.	D	18.	B
4.	D	19.	B
5.	B	20.	B
6.	A	21.	A
7.	B	22.	D
8.	B	23.	B
9.	D	24.	A
10.	A	25.	A
11.	D	26.	C
12.	D	27.	B
13.	C	28.	D
14.	C	29.	B
15.	C	30.	C

EXAMINATION SECTION

TEST 1

DIRECTIONS: Each question or incomplete statement is followed by several suggested answers or completions. Select the one that BEST answers the question or completes the statement. *PRINT THE LETTER OF THE CORRECT ANSWER IN THE SPACE AT THE RIGHT.*

1. The product of the readings of an AC voltmeter and AC ammeter is called 1.____
   A. apparent power
   B. true power
   C. power factor
   D. current power

2. What is the basic unit of electrical power? 2.____
   A. Ohm
   B. Watt
   C. Volt
   D. Ampere

3. What is the term used to express the amount of electrical energy stored in an electrostatic field? 3.____
   A. Joules
   B. Coulombs
   C. Watts
   D. Volts

4. What device is used to store electrical energy in an electrostatic field? 4.____
   A. Battery
   B. Transformer
   C. Capacitor
   D. Inductor

5. What formula would determine the inductive reactance of a coil if frequency and coil inductance are known? 5.____
   $X_L =$
   A. πfL
   B. 2πfL
   C. 1/2π
   D. 1/R2+X2

6. What is the term for the out-of-phase power associated with inductors and capacitors? 6.____
   A. Effective power
   B. True power
   C. Peak envelope power
   D. Reactive power

7. What determines the strength of the magnetic field around a conductor? 7.____
   The
   A. resistance divided by the current
   B. ratio of the current to the resistance
   C. diameter of the conductor
   D. amount of current

8. What will produce a magnetic field? 8.____
   A. A DC source not connected to a circuit
   B. The presence of a voltage across a capacitor
   C. A current flowing through a conductor
   D. The force that drives current through a resistor

9. When induced currents produce expanding magnetic fields around conductors in a direction that opposes the original magnetic field, this is known as _____ law.
   A. Lenz's   B. Gilbert's   C. Maxwell's   D. Norton's

   9._____

10. The opposition to the creation of magnetic lines of force in a magnetic circuit is known as
    A. eddy currents   B. hysteresis   C. permeability   D. reluctance

    10._____

11. What is meant by the term *back EMF*? A(n) _____ the applied EFM.
    A. current equal to
    B. opposing EMF equal to R times C (RC) percent of
    C. voltage that opposes
    D. current that opposes

    11._____

12. Permeability is defined as
    A. the magnetic field created by a conductor wound on a laminated core and carrying current
    B. ratio of magnetic flux density in a substance to the magnetizing force that produces it
    C. polarized molecular alignment in a ferromagnetic material while under the influence of a magnetizing force
    D. none of these

    12._____

13. What metal is usually employed as a sacrificial anode for corrosion control purposes?
    A. Platinum bushing   B. Lead bar
    C. Zinc bar   D. Brass rod

    13._____

14. What is the relative dielectric constant for air?
    A. 1   B. 2   C. 4   D. 0

    14._____

15. Which metal object may be least affected by galvanic corrosion when submerged in seawater?
    A. Aluminum outdrive   B. Bronze through-hull
    C. Exposed lead keel   D. Stainless steel propeller shaft

    15._____

16. Skin effect is the phenomenon where
    A. RF current flows in a thinner layer of the conductor, closer to the surface, as frequency increases
    B. RF current flows in a thinner layer of the conductor, closer to the surface, as frequency decreases
    C. thermal effects on the surface of the conductor increase the impedance
    D. thermal effects on the surface of the conductor decrease the impedance

    16._____

17. Corrosion resulting from electric current flow between dissimilar metals is called
    A. electrolysis   B. stray current corrosion
    C. oxygen starvation corrosion   D. galvanic corrosion

    17._____

18. Which of these will be most useful for insulation at UHF frequencies? 18.____
    A. Rubber
    B. Mica
    C. Wax impregnated paper
    D. Lead

19. What formula would calculate the total inductance of inductors in series? 19.____
    $L_T =$
    A. L_1/L_2
    B. L_1+L_2
    C. $1/L_1+L_2$
    D. $1/L_1 \times L_2$

20. Good conductors with minimum resistance have what type of electrons? 20.____
    A. Few free electrons
    B. No electrons
    C. Some free electrons
    D. Many free electrons

21. Which of the four groups of metals listed below are the BEST low-resistance conductors? 21.____
    A. Gold, silver, and copper
    B. Stainless steel, bronze, and lead
    C. Iron, lead, and nickel
    D. Bronze, zinc, and manganese

22. What is the purpose of a bypass capacitor? 22.____
    It
    A. increases the resonant frequency of the circuit
    B. removes direct current from the circuit by shunting DC to ground
    C. removes alternating current by providing a low impedance path to ground
    D. forms part of an impedance transforming circuit

23. How would you calculate the total capacitance of three capacitors in parallel? 23.____
    $C_T =$
    A. $C_1+C_2/C_1-C_2+C_3$
    B. $C_1+C_2+C_3$
    C. $C_1+C_2/C_1 \times C_2+C_3$
    D. $1/C_1+1/C_2+1/C_3$

24. How might you reduce the inductance of an antenna coil? 24.____
    A. Add additional turns
    B. Add more core permeability
    C. Reduce the number of turns
    D. Compress the coil turns

25. What are the two most commonly-used specifications for a junction diode? 25.____
    Maximum
    A. forward current and capacitance
    B. reverse current and PIV (peak inverse voltage)
    C. reverse current and capacitance
    D. forward current and PIV (peak inverse voltage)

26. What limits the maximum forward current in a junction diode? 26.____
    The
    A. peak inverse voltage (PIV)
    B. junction temperature
    C. forward voltage
    D. back EMF

27. MOSFETs are manufactured with this protective device built into their gate to protect the device from static charges and excessive voltages:
    A. Schottky diode
    B. Metal oxide varistor (MOV)
    C. Zener diode
    D. Tunnel diode

    27.____

28. What are the two basic types of junction field-effect transistors?
    A. N-channel and P-channel
    B. High power and low power
    C. MOSFET and GaAsFET
    D. Silicon FET and germanium FET

    28.____

29. A common emitter amplifier has
    A. lower input impedance than a common base
    B. more voltage gain than a common collector
    C. less current gain than a common base
    D. less voltage gain than a common collector

    29.____

30. How does the input impedance of a field-effect transistor compare with that of a bipolar transistor?
    A. An FET has high input impedance; a bipolar transistor has low input impedance.
    B. One cannot compare input impedance without first knowing the supply voltage.
    C. An FET has low input impedance; a bipolar transistor has high input impedance.
    D. The input impedance of FETs and bipolar transistors is the same.

    30.____

KEY (CORRECT ANSWERS)

1.	A	11.	C	21.	A
2.	B	12.	B	22.	C
3.	A	13.	C	23.	B
4.	C	14.	A	24.	C
5.	B	15.	D	25.	D
6.	D	16.	A	26.	B
7.	D	17.	D	27.	C
8.	C	18.	B	28.	A
9.	A	19.	B	29.	B
10.	D	20.	D	30.	A

TEST 2

DIRECTIONS: Each question or incomplete statement is followed by several suggested answers or completions. Select the one that BEST answers the question or completes the statement. *PRINT THE LETTER OF THE CORRECT ANSWER IN THE SPACE AT THE RIGHT.*

1. The unit of inductance is
   A. henry B. joule C. coulomb D. ohm

   1._____

2. The ratio of current through a conductor to the voltage which produces it is
   A. inductance
   B. conductance
   C. resistance
   D. none of the above

   2._____

3. The product of the number of turns and the current in amperes used to describe relative magnitude is
   A. ampere turns
   B. joules per second
   C. push-pull convergence
   D. dissipation collection

   3._____

4. The property of a conductor or coil which causes a voltage to be developed across its terminals when the number of magnetic lines of force in the circuit or coil is changed is
   A. capacitance
   B. inductance
   C. conductance
   D. none of the above

   4._____

5. The charge of electricity which passes a given point in one second when a current of one ampere is flowing is
   A. coulomb
   B. joule
   C. watt
   D. none of the above

   5._____

6. C = capacity in farads. Q = the measure of the quantity of charge of electricity in coulombs. E = the applied voltage. So, Q = CE
   A. determines the quantity of charge in a capacitor
   B. determines the Q of a circuit
   C. both A and B
   D. none of the above

   6._____

7. An AC ammeter indicates _____ values of current.
   A. effective (TRM)
   B. effective (RMS)
   C. peak
   D. average

   7._____

8. By what factor must the voltage of an AC circuit, as indicated on the scale of an AC voltmeter, be multiplied to obtain the peak voltage value?
   A. 0.707 B. 0.9 C. 1.414 D. 3.14

   8._____

9. What is the RMS voltage at a common household electrical power outlet?
   A. 3310V AC
   B. 82.7-V AC
   C. 165.5-V AC
   D. 117-V AC

   9._____

35

2 (#2)

10. What is the easiest voltage amplitude to measure by viewing a pure sine wave signal on an oscilloscope? 10.____
    A. Peak-to-peak B. RMS C. Average D. DC

11. By what factor must the voltage measured in an AC circuit, as indicated on the scale of an AC voltmeter, be multiplied to obtain the average voltage value? 11.____
    A. 0.707 B. 1.414 C. 0.9 D. 3.14

12. What is the peak voltage at a common household electrical outlet? 12.____
    A. 234 volts B. 117 volts C. 331 volts D. 165.5 volts

13. What is a sine wave? 13.____
    A. A constant-voltage, varying-current wave
    B. A wave whose amplitude at any given instant can be represented by the projection of a point on a wheel rotating at a uniform speed
    C. A wave following the laws of the trigonometric tangent function
    D. A wave whose polarity changes in a random manner

14. How many degrees are there in one complete sine wave cycle? 14.____
    A. 90 degrees
    B. 270 degrees
    C. 180 degrees
    D. 360 degrees

15. What type of wave is made up of sine waves of the fundamental frequency and all the odd harmonics? 15.____
    A. Square B. Sine C. Cosine D. Tangent

16. What is the description of a square wave? 16.____
    A wave
    A. with only 300 degrees in one cycle
    B. whose periodic function is always negative
    C. whose periodic function is always positive
    D. that abruptly changes back and forth between two voltage levels and stays at these levels for equal amounts of time

17. What type of wave is made up of sine waves at the fundamental frequency and all the harmonics? 17.____
    A. Sawtooth wave
    B. Square wave
    C. Sine wave
    D. Cosine wave

18. What type of wave is characterized by a rise time significantly faster than the fall time (or vice versa)? 18.____
    A. Cosine wave
    B. Square wave
    C. Sawtooth wave
    D. Sine wave

19. What is the term used to identi8fy an AC voltage that would cause the same heating in a resistor as a corresponding value of DC voltage? 19.____
    A. Cosine voltage
    B. Power factor
    C. Root mean square (RMS)
    D. Average voltage

20. What happens to reactive power in a circuit that has both inductors and capacitors? 20.____
    A. It is dissipated as heat in the circuit.
    B. It alternates between magnetic and electric fields and is not dissipated.
    C. It is dissipated as inductive and capacitive fields.
    D. It is dissipated as kinetic energy within the circuit.

21. Halving the cross-sectional area of a conductor will _____ the resistance. 21.____
    A. not affect   B. quarter   C. double   D. halve

22. Which of the following groups is correct for listing common materials in order of descending conductivity? 22.____
    A. Silver, copper, aluminum, iron, and lead
    B. Lead, iron, silver, aluminum, and copper
    C. Iron, silver, aluminum, copper, and lead
    D. Silver, aluminum, iron, lead, and copper

23. How do you compute true power (power dissipated in the circuit) in a circuit where AC voltage and current are out of phase? 23.____
    A. Multiple RMS voltage times RMS current
    B. Subtract apparent power from the power factor
    C. Divide apparent power by the power factor
    D. Multiple apparent power times the power factor

24. Assuming a power source to have a fixed value of internal resistance, maximum power will be transferred to the load when the 24.____
    A. load impedance is greater than the source impedance
    B. load impedance equals the internal impedance of the source
    C. load impedance is less than the source impedance
    D. fixed values of internal impedance are not relative to the power source

25. What is the total resistance of a parallel circuit consisting of a 10 ohm branch and a 25 ohm branch? 25.____
    A. 6 ohms   B. 10.3 ohm   C. 7.0 ohms   D. 7.14 ohms

26. The current through two resistors in series is 3A. Resistance #1 is 50 ohms; resistance #2 drops 50V across its terminals. What is the total voltage? 26.____
    A. 200V   B. 220V   C. 110V   D. 180V

27. An 18 ohm and a 15 ohm resistor are connected in parallel; a 36 ohm resistor is connected in series with this combination; a 22 ohm resistor is connected in parallel with this total combination. The total current is 5A. What current is flowing in the 15 ohm resistor? 27.____
    A. 0.908A   B. 1.000A   C. 1.908A   D. 0.809A

28. A circuit passes 3A. The internal resistance of the source is 2 ohms. The total resistance is 50 ohms. What is the terminal voltage of the source? 28.____
    A. 150V   B. 100V   C. 110V   D. 240V

4 (#2)

29. A relay coil has 500 ohms resistance and operates on 125 mA. What value of resistance should be connected in series with it to operate from 110 VDC?   29.____
    A. 380 ohms
    B. 400 ohms
    C. 200 ohms
    D. None of the above

30. Given: Input power to a receiver is 75 watts. How much power does the receiver consume in 24 hours of continuous operation?   30.____
    A. 1800 watthours
    B. 1.80 kilowatt hours
    C. A and B
    D. None of the above

KEY (CORRECT ANSWERS)

1.	A	11.	C	21.	C
2.	B	12.	D	22.	A
3.	A	13.	B	23.	D
4.	B	14.	D	24.	B
5.	A	15.	A	25.	D
6.	A	16.	D	26.	A
7.	B	17.	A	27.	A
8.	C	18.	C	28.	A
9.	D	19.	C	29.	A
10.	A	20.	B	30.	C

EXAMINATION SECTION
TEST 1

DIRECTIONS: Each question or incomplete statement is followed by several suggested answers or completions. Select the one that BEST answers the question or completes the statement. *PRINT THE LETTER OF THE CORRECT ANSWER IN THE SPACE AT THE RIGHT.*

Questions 1-16.

DIRECTIONS: Questions 1 through 16 deal with graphical symbols of electrical items as recommended by the ANSI (ex-ASA). For each item, select the proper graphical symbol and print the letter corresponding to it.

1. Telephone switchboard

 A. 6   B. 16   C. 17   D. 18

2. Exit light wall outlet

 A. 5   B. 12   C. 15   D. 16

3. City fire alarm station

 A. 19   B. 21   C. 22   D. 23

4. Electric door opener

 A. 9   B. 10   C. 11   D. 15

5. Duplex convenience outlet

 A. 9   B. 10   C. 15   D. 24

6. Range outlet

 A. 3   B. 6   C. 13   D. 14

7. Push button

 A. 5   B. 8   C. 11   D. 12

8. Power panel

 A. 1   B. 2   C. 3   D. 4

1. ____

2. ____

3. ____

4. ____

5. ____

6. ____

7. ____

8. ____

2 (#1)

9. Four-way switch

   A. 4 B. 13 C. 14 D. 16

10. Controller

   A. 3 B. 4 C. 5 D. 9

11. Lighting panel

   A. 1 B. 2 C. 3 D. 4

12. Buzzer

   A. 3 B. 5 C. 8 D. 11

13. Isolating switch

   A. 3 B. 5 C. 9 D. 10

14. Interconnecting telephone

   A. 13 B. 14 C. 17 D. 18

15. Fire alarm central station

   A. 21 B. 22 C. 23 D. 26

16. Clock outlet

   A. 9 B. 10 C. 15 D. 26

18. ◁

19. S_F

20. S_{MC}

21. FA

22. F

23. ⊠

24. ─○

25. ≡○ 3

26. Ⓒ

9.____

10.____

11.____

12.____

13.____

14.____

15.____

16.____

17. A riser diagram is an electrical drawing which would give information about the

    A. voltage drop in feeders
    B. size of feeders and panel loads
    C. external connections to equipment
    D. sequence of operation of devices and equipment

18. When a contractor fails to adhere to an approved progress schedule, he should

    A. revise the schedule without delay
    B. ask for an extension of time on account of delays
    C. adopt such additional means and methods of construction as will make up for the time lost
    D. take no immediate action with the hope that sufficient time will be available later on that will assure the completion in accordance with the schedule

19. The usual contract for work includes a section entitled, *Instructions to Bidders,* which states that the

    A. contractor agrees that he has made his own examination and will make no claims for damages on account of errors or omissions
    B. contractor shall not make claims for damages of any discrepancy, error or omission in any plans
    C. estimates of quantities and calculations are guaranteed by the Board to be correct and are deemed to be a representation of the conditions affecting the work
    D. plans, measurements, dimensions, and conditions under which the work is to be performed are guaranteed by the Board

20. The purpose of performing a dielectric test on a sample of oil taken from the casing of an oil-filled power transformer is to determine the

    A. viscosity
    B. insulating quality
    C. flashpoint
    D. extent of contamination

21. A neon test lamp can be used to test

    A. the field intensity of a relay magnet
    B. the phase rotation of a source of supply
    C. whether a supply source is A.C. or D.C.
    D. the power factor of a source of supply

22. The size, in circular mils, of a wire whose diameter is known can be calculated by

    A. multiplying the diameter in mils by $\pi/4$
    B. squaring the diameter in mils
    C. squaring the diameter in mils and multiplying the product by $\pi/4$
    D. squaring the diameter in inches

23. The short time rating and the continuous rating of a given piece of electrical machinery differ, but both are based on the

    A. cost of energy
    B. line potential

C. power factor of the machine
D. temperature rise of the machine

24. A lump sum type of contract may require the contractor to submit a schedule of unit prices.
The BEST reason for this is that it

   A. prevents the lump sum from being too high
   B. simplifies the selection of the lowest bidder
   C. enables the estimators to check the total cost
   D. provides a means of making equitable partial payments

24._____

25. In assigning his men to various jobs, the BEST principle for a supervisor to follow is to

   A. study the men's abilities and assign them accordingly
   B. rotate a man from job to job until you find one which he can do well
   C. assign each of them a job and let them adjust to it in their own way
   D. assume that men appointed to the position can do all parts of the work equally well

25._____

KEY (CORRECT ANSWERS)

1.	D	11.	A
2.	B	12.	B
3.	D	13.	A
4.	B	14.	C
5.	D	15.	A
6.	C	16.	D
7.	B	17.	B
8.	B	18.	C
9.	D	19.	A
10.	B	20.	C

21.	C
22.	B
23.	D
24.	D
25.	A

TEST 2

DIRECTIONS: Each question or incomplete statement is followed by several suggested answers or completions. Select the one that BEST answers the question or completes the statement. *PRINT THE LETTER OF THE CORRECT ANSWER IN THE SPACE AT THE RIGHT.*

Questions 1-8.

DIRECTIONS: Questions 1 through 8 are to be answered in accordance with the requirements of the electrical code, assuming normal procedures. Do NOT consider exceptions which are granted by special permission.

1. The MINIMUM size of A.W.G. wire which may be used on a 15-ampere branch circuit is

   A. 10 B. 12 C. 14 D. 16

2. Conductors supplying an individual motor whose full-load current is 100 amperes should have a MINIMUM carrying capacity of _____ amperes.

   A. 100 B. 115 C. 125 D. 150

3. The MINIMUM rating of a service switch is _____ amperes.

   A. 30 B. 60 C. 100 D. 200

4. In the installation of fluorescent fixtures, the MAXIMUM number of single or two-lamp type auxiliaries which can be placed on any single fifteen-ampere branch circuit is

   A. 10 B. 12 C. 15 D. 18

5. Where rubber-covered conductors are used in a conduit, the MINIMUM radius of the curve of the inner edge of any field bend, in terms of the internal diameter of the conduit, shall not be less than _____ times.

   A. 4 B. 6 C. 8 D. 10

6. Except for fixture wire of MI cable, single conductors of No. 6 A.W.G. or smaller intended for use as identified conductors of circuits shall have an outer identification of

   A. green
   B. black
   C. white or natural gray
   D. gray with a yellow marker throughout its length

7. Motor running protective devices, other than fuses, should have a continuous current-carrying capacity, in terms of the full load current rating of the motor, of AT LEAST

   A. 100% B. 115% C. 120% D. 125%

8. The one of the following which should ALWAYS be used as the grounding electrode, where available, is a

   A. driven non-ferrous metallic rod
   B. buried plate with an area of 2 sq.ft.
   C. driven iron rod with a resistance of 25 ohms
   D. continuous metallic underground water piping system

9. The MAIN reason for requiring written job reports is to

   A. avoid the necessity of oral orders
   B. develop better methods of doing the work
   C. provide a permanent record of what was done
   D. increase the amount of work that can be done

10. Of the following items, the one which should NOT be included in a proposed work schedule is

    A. a schedule of hourly wage rates and supplementary benefits
    B. an estimated time required for delivery of materials and equipment
    C. the anticipated commencement and completion of the various operations
    D. the sequence and inter-relationship of various operations with those of related contracts

11. The closed circuit is used primarily in communication and fire alarm systems to indicate, by various or audible means, which of the following abnormal circuit conditions?

    A. Open
    B. Ground
    C. Overload
    D. Direct short

12. A Board specification states that access panels to suspended ceiling will be of metal. The MAIN reason for providing access panels is to

    A. improve the insulation of the ceiling
    B. improve the appearance of the building
    C. make it easier to construct the building
    D. make it easier to maintain the building

13. The one of the following which is a successful means of decreasing electrolysis in underground metal pipes is to

    A. use galvanized pipe
    B. insert occasional insulating joints in the pipes
    C. keep the voltage drop in the ground return circuit over 15 volts
    D. coat the pipe with tar for 6 inches above and 6 inches below the point where it enters the ground

14. The abbreviation *MCM* placed next to a feeder cable in a wiring diagram would indicate the

    A. microamperes per circular mil
    B. area of the cable in millions of circular mils
    C. area of the cable in thousands of circular mils
    D. resistance of the cable in microhms per circular-mil-ft.

15. Which one of the following is the PRIMARY object in drawing up a set of specifications for materials to be purchased?

    A. Control of quality
    B. Outline of intended use
    C. Establishment of standard sizes
    D. Location and method of inspection

16. The marking or lettering that indicates a conductor having moisture-and-heat resistance thermoplastic covering and which may be used in both dry and wet locations is 16._____

   A. RHW   B. SB   C. THW   D. TW

17. In performing field inspectional work, an inspector is the contact man between the public and the authority, and it is his job to secure compliance through the maximum utilization of persuasion and education and the minimum application of coercion. 17._____
    According to the above statement, an inspector performing inspectional duties should

   A. seek to obtain voluntary compliance and use coercion only as a last resort
   B. be conciliatory on all issues of non-compliance and not take an attitude of firmness and authority
   C. maintain a strictly impersonal attitude in the exercise of his duties at all times
   D. use the threat of legal action to secure conformance with specified requirements

18. In a polarized interior lighting system, the 18._____

   A. base of the lamp sockets is connected to the identified wire
   B. branch circuit light switch is connected to the identifying wire
   C. screwshells of the lamp sockets are connected to the identified wire
   D. branch circuit light switch is connected to the screwshell of the lamp socket

19. If a supervisor finds a discrepancy between the plans and specifications, he should 19._____

   A. always follow the plans
   B. ask for an interpretation
   C. always follow the specifications
   D. follow the plans if the difference is in dimensions

20. The BEST way to evaluate the overall state of completion of a construction project is to check the progress estimate against the 20._____

   A. inspection work sheet
   B. construction schedule
   C. inspector's checklist
   D. equipment maintenance schedule

21. Two-phase power may be converted to 3-phase power, or vice versa, by using which of the following transformer connections? 21._____

   A. Scott   B. Delta-wye
   C. Open delta   D. Autotransformer

22. The CHIEF purpose in preparing an outline for a report is usually to insure that 22._____

   A. the report will be grammatically correct
   B. every point will be given equal emphasis
   C. principal and secondary points will be properly integrated
   D. the language of the report will be of the same level and include the same technical terms

23. A contractor on a large construction project USUALLY receives partial payments based on

    A. estimates of completed work
    B. actual cost of materials delivered and work completed
    C. estimates of material delivered and not paid for by the contractor
    D. the breakdown estimate submitted after the contract was signed and prorated over the estimated duration of the contract

24. In testing insulation resistance, the MAIN reason that the use of a megger is *preferable* to the use of an ordinary ohmmeter is that a megger

    A. is more rugged
    B. does not require constant care
    C. has a lower internal resistance
    D. usually operates at the proper voltage

25. In order to avoid disputes over payments for extra work in a contract for construction, the BEST procedure to follow would be to

    A. have contractor submit work progress reports daily
    B. insert a special clause in the contract specifications
    C. have a representative on the job at all times to verify conditions
    D. allocate a certain percentage of the cost of the job to cover such expenses

KEY (CORRECT ANSWERS)

1. B
2. C
3. C
4. C
5. B

6. C
7. B
8. D
9. C
10. A

11. A
12. D
13. B
14. C
15. A

16. C
17. A
18. C
19. B
20. B

21. A
22. C
23. A
24. D
25. C

TEST 3

DIRECTIONS: Each question or incomplete statement is followed by several suggested answers or completions. Select the one that BEST answers the question or completes the statement. *PRINT THE LETTER OF THE CORRECT ANSWER IN THE SPACE AT THE RIGHT.*

1. During the actual construction work, the CHIEF value of a construction schedule is to   1.____

   A. insure that the work will be done on time
   B. reveal whether production is falling behind
   C. show how much equipment and material is required for the project
   D. furnish data as to the methods and techniques of construction operations

2. Prior to the installation of equipment called for in the specifications, the contractor is usually required to submit for approval   2.____

   A. sets of shop drawings
   B. a set of revised specifications
   C. a detailed description of the methods of work to be used
   D. a complete list of skilled and unskilled tradesmen he proposes to use

3. An inspector inspecting a large building under construction inspected lighting fixtures at 9 A.M. and electrical feeders at 10 A.M., machine connections at 11 A.M., and did his office work in the afternoon. He followed the same pattern daily for months.
   This procedure is   3.____

   A. *bad,* because not enough time is devoted to important electrical feeders
   B. *bad,* because the tradesmen know when the inspections occur
   C. *good,* because it is methodical and he does not miss any of the trades
   D. *good,* because it gives equal amount of time to the important trades

4. A rule of thumb for calculating the area of copper conductors in C.M. as given in the AWG tables is that for every _____ size, the wire cross section _____.   4.____

   A. second gage of larger; doubles
   B. second gage of larger; increases four times
   C. third gage of smaller; is halved
   D. third gage of smaller; is one-third

5. The drawing which should be used as a legal reference when checking completed construction work is the _____ drawing(s).   5.____

   A. contract   B. assembly
   C. working or shop   D. preliminary

6. The motor starting device commonly called a compensator is actually a(n)   6.____

   A. rheostat   B. potentiometer
   C. auto-transformer   D. capacitor

7. The BEST way for a supervisor to determine whether a new employee is learning his work properly is to   7.____

A. ask the other men how this man is making out
B. question him directly on details of the work
C. assume that if he asks no questions he knows the work
D. inspect and follow up on the work which is assigned to him

Questions 8-13.

DIRECTIONS: Questions 8 through 13 refer to the circuit drawn below.

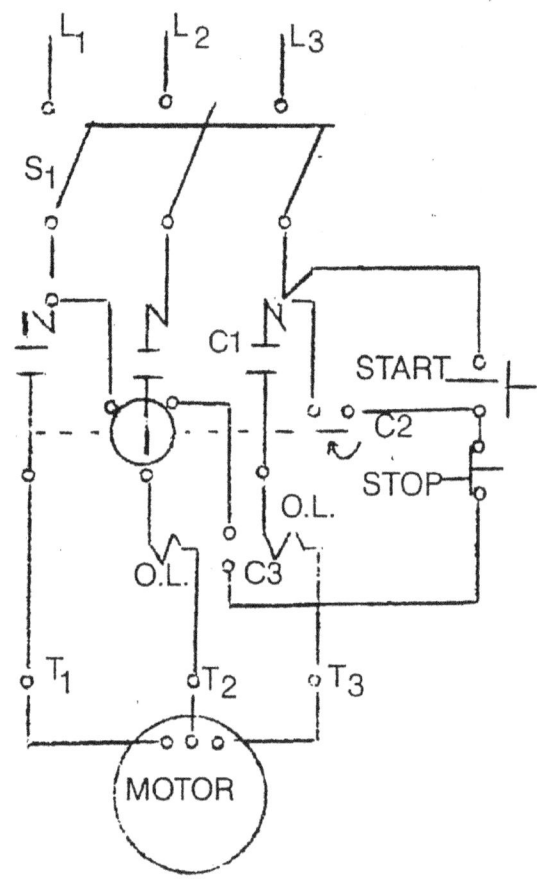

8. The circuitry shown is called a(n)

    A. D.C. motor controller
    B. reduced voltage starter
    C. two-speed motor control
    D. across-the-line starter

9. The circuit element indicated by C_1 is a

    A. capacitor
    B. circuit breaker
    C. pair of contacts which is normally open
    D. pair of start button contacts

8.____

9.____

10. If the motor is of the three-phase induction type, the incoming power is MOST likely

   A. plus and minus 115 volts D.C.
   B. 115 volts A.C. with neutral
   C. 208 volts A.C. line-to-line
   D. 230 volts D.C. with neutral

11. The PROPER designation for line switch S_1 is

   A. SPST   B. 3PDT   C. 3TSP   D. 3TDP

12. The O.L. relays are in the circuitry to

   A. protect the motor from overvoltages
   B. keep the stop button in after it has been depressed
   C. allow the motor to be operated on two lines if desired
   D. interrupt the contactor holding circuit on sustained overloads

13. The purpose of contact C_2 is to

   A. hold the start button in after it has been depressed
   B. hold the contactor in when the line voltages drop too low
   C. hold the contactor in after the start button has been depressed
   D. de-energize the contactor solenoid when the stop button is depressed

14. One ADVANTAGE of fluorescent lamps over incandescent lamps is that they

   A. are easier to handle
   B. are more efficient
   C. have simpler wiring circuits
   D. are not affected by temperature changes

15. To control a light fixture from three different locations, it is necessary to use _____ switches.

   A. one 4-way and two 3-way   B. three 3-way
   C. three 2-way   D. three single-pole

16. Good inspection methods require that the inspector

   A. be observant and check all details
   B. constantly check with the engineer who designed the school
   C. apply specifications according to his interpretations
   D. permit slight job violations to establish good public relations

17. Assume you are recommending in a report to your superior that a radical change in a standard maintenance procedure should be adopted.
    Of the following, the MOST important information to be included in this report is

   A. a list of the reasons for making this change
   B. the names of the other supervisors who favor the change
   C. a complete description of the present procedure
   D. amount of training time needed for the new procedure

18. A fixed amount of money is generally withheld from the contractor for a definite period after the completion of construction.
    The BEST reason for this is

    A. that the money will be available for taxes due
    B. to penalize the contractor for poor work
    C. that it is a security for the repair of any defective work
    D. that the money will be available for modifications in the design of the structure

    18._____

19. The frequency with which job reports are submitted should depend MAINLY on

    A. how comprehensive the report has to be
    B. the amount of information in the report
    C. the availability of an experienced man to write the report
    D. the importance of changes in the information included in the report

    19._____

20. The use of groups of combinations of conductors in the same conduit will

    A. decrease conductor resistance
    B. be allowed for circuit voltages not exceeding 250V
    C. upgrade the current-carrying capacity of the conductors
    D. downgrade the current-carrying capacity of the conductors

    20._____

KEY (CORRECT ANSWERS)

1.	B	11.	A
2.	A	12.	D
3.	B	13.	C
4.	C	14.	B
5.	A	15.	A
6.	C	16.	A
7.	B	17.	A
8.	D	18.	C
9.	C	19.	D
10.	C	20.	D

EXAMINATION SECTION
TEST 1

DIRECTIONS: Each question or incomplete statement is followed by several suggested answers or completions. Select the one that BEST answers the question or completes the statement. *PRINT THE LETTER OF THE CORRECT ANSWER IN THE SPACE AT THE RIGHT.*

1. A piece of No. 1/0 emery cloth should be used to sand the commutator of a D.C. dynamo   1.____

   A. when there is sparking at the brushes
   B. under no conditions
   C. when the commutator has a "chocolate" color
   D. only when the commutator has ridges

2. Compound D.C. generators connected in parallel are *generally* provided with   2.____

   A. 3 brushes   B. an equalizer
   C. no voltage relays   D. armature resistors

3. As compared with other types of A.C. motors, the advantage of the squirrel cage motor lies in its   3.____

   A. high starting torque   B. high power factor
   C. constant speed   D. simplicity

4. A counter E.M.F. starter is so named because   4.____

   A. the accelerating contactor has a high counter E.M.F.
   B. the accelerating relay depends upon the armature terminal voltage for operation
   C. it is used only on motors that build up a high C.E.M.F.
   D. it stops the motor by means of C.E.M.F.

5. There shall NOT be more than _____ quarter bends or their equivalent from outlet to outlet in rigid conduit.   5.____

   A. 3   B. 4   C. 5   D. 6

6. Armored cable may be imbedded in masonry in buildings under construction *provided*   6.____

   A. it is type AC   B. it is fastened securely
   C. it is type ACL   D. special permission is obtained

7. An armature core is laminated in order to reduce   7.____

   A. hysteresis loss   B. eddy current loss
   C. hysteresis and eddy current loss   D. impedance loss

8. The MOST efficient size of the "white" fluorescent lamps is   8.____

   A. 15 watts   B. 30 watts   C. 40 watts   D. 100 watts

9. Condensers are placed in parallel with fluorescent glow switches in order to   9.____

   A. reduce radio interference   B. reduce the arc
   C. compensate the power factor   D. increase the lamp life

10. The SMALLEST size wire that may be used on fire alarm systems is No. _____   10.____

    A. 18   B. 16   C. 14   D. 12

11. Under the National Electric Code, a 3-way switch is classified as a(n)   11.____

    A. single pole switch   B. double pole switch
    C. 3-way switch   D. electrolier switch

12. A capacitor start-and-run motor may be reversed by reversing the   12.____

    A. running and starting capacitor leads
    B. main winding leads
    C. line leads
    D. centrifugal switch leads

13. Opening a series field circuit while a compound motor is operating, will cause   13.____

    A. the motor to stop   B. no noticeable change
    C. the motor to race   D. the motor to slow down

14. Transformers for neon signs shall have a secondary voltage NOT exceeding   14.____

    A. 10,000 volts   B. 15,000 volts
    C. 20,000 volts   D. 25,000 volts

15. A capacitor of 10 ohms reactance and zero ohms resistance is connected in series with   15.____
    an inductance of 7 ohms reactance and 4 ohms resistance. The total impedance is

    A. 5 ohms   B. 7 ohms   C. 17 ohms   D. 21 ohms

16. The BEST way to start a large shunt motor is with a   16.____

    A. strong field   B. weak field
    C. rheostat in series with the armature and the field
    D. starting compensator.

17. If an A.C. motor draws 50 amps., full load, the thermal cutout should be set at   17.____

    A. 75 amps.   B. 50 amps.   C. 62.5 amps.   D. 75 amps.

18. Using 1:1 ratio transformers at a given primary voltage, the HIGHEST secondary voltage   18.____
    may be obtained by connecting them

    A. Wye primary and Delta secondary
    B. Delta primary and Delta secondary
    C. Wye primary and Wye secondary
    D. Delta primary and Wye secondary

19. In an A.C. fire alarm system, the number of gongs allowed on a circuit is   19.____

    A. 10   B. 12   C. 14   D. 20

20. Appliance branch circuit wires shall be NO smaller than No.   20.____

    A. 8   B. 10   C. 12   D. 14

21. A current of 2 amperes in a resistor of 10 ohms will use electrical energy at the rate of _____ watts.

    A. 10 B. 20 C. 40 D. 80

22. 20-, 40-, and 50-ohm resistances are connected in series across a 110-volt D.C. supply; the current through the 20-ohm resistance is

    A. 5.5 amperes B. 1 ampere C. 2.2 ampers D. 2.75 amperes

23. An electric circuit has four resistances of 20,6,30, and 12 ohms in parallel with each other. The combined resistance, in ohms, is

    A. 300 B. 30 C. 3 D. .3

24. The load for general illumination in apartment and multifamily dwellings is based on

    A. 1 1/2 watts per square foot of floor area
    B. 2 watts per square foot of floor area
    C. 3 watts per square foot of floor area
    D. 4 watts per square foot of floor area

25. Ventilation of battery rooms is necessary to

    A. keep the batteries cool
    B. prevent accumulation of explosive gases
    C. prevent deterioration of insulation
    D. supply oxygen to the room

KEYS (CORRECT ANSWERS)

1. B		11. A	
2. B		12. B	
3. D		13. A	
4. B		14. B	
5. B		15. A	
6. C		16. A	
7. B		17. C	
8. C		18. D	
9. A		19. A	
10. C		20. C	

21. B
22. B
23. C
24. B
25. B

TEST 2

DIRECTIONS: Each question or incomplete statement is followed by several suggested answers or completions. Select the one that BEST answers the question or completes the statement. *PRINT THE LETTER OF THE CORRECT ANSWER IN THE SPACE AT THE RIGHT.*

1. Dynamic braking is obtained in a motor by means of

    A. a magnetic brake
    B. a resistance connected across the armature after the current is disconnected
    C. reversing the armature
    D. reversing the field

2. The reason for using flux when soldering splices is to

    A. lower the melting point of the solder
    B. cause the joint to heat rapidly
    C. reduce the oxide on the wires
    D. prevent corrosion of the wires after soldering

3. A good ammeter should have

    A. very high resistance
    B. very low resistance
    C. low resistance
    D. high resistance

4. A good voltmeter should have

    A. very high resistance
    B. very low resistance
    C. low resistance
    D. high resistance

5. The MOST efficient type of polyphase motor to install for a large, slow speed, direct connected machine would be a

    A. wound rotor induction motor
    B. squirrel cage induction motor
    C. synchronous motor
    D. high torque induction motor

6. Mercury is added to the gas in a neon tube in order to produce the color

    A. gold   B. blue   C. white   D. red

7. An electromotive force will be built up in a conductor if it is moving

    A. in the same direction as magnetic lines of force
    B. in the opposite direction
    C. at right angles to the lines of force
    D. in any direction

8. The BEST choice of an A.C. motor to produce a high starting torque would be a

    A. synchronous motor
    B. split phase motor
    C. shaded pole motor
    D. wound rotor induction motor

9. The speed of a squirrel cage motor may be reduced by   9.____

   A. inserting a line resistance
   B. inserting a line reactance
   C. increasing the number of poles
   D. decreasing the number of poles

10. Three-point starting boxes provide for   10.____

    A. speed regulation   B. no field release
    C. no voltage release   D. phase reversal

11. If the #10 wire feeding a circuit were replaced with a #7 wire, the voltage drop would be reduced, *approximately*,   11.____

    A. 100%   B. 33%   C. 66%   D. 50%

12. Theatre footlight and border light branch circuits shall be so wired that in NO case will they carry *more than* _____ amperes.   12.____

    A. 10   B. 14   C. 20   D. 25

13. Which of the following is the outstanding feature of the Edison storage battery?   13.____

    A. A continued short circuit will not ruin the battery
    B. The lead plates are smaller
    C. It has a greater voltage output per cell
    D. It is less expensive than the automobile lead storage battery

14. An impedance coil is connected into a telephone circuit in the   14.____

    A. ringing circuit   B. talking circuit
    C. ringing and talking circuit
    D. secondary side of the induction coil

15. An electro reset annunciator has   15.____

    A. two coils per figure   B. one coil per figure
    C. one coil and one permanent magnet   D. manual reset arrangement

16. Locking relays may be used in   16.____

    A. open circuit burglar alarm systems only
    B. closed circuit burglar alarm systems only
    C. any type of burglar alarm system
    D. no burglar alarm system

17. The unit or electrical inductance is the   17.____

    A. henry   B. farad   C. joule   D. mho

18. The method used in calculating the total of resistances in series is NEAREST to that used in calculating   18.____

    A. condensers in series   B. inductances in parallel
    C. condensers in parallel   D. impedances in parallel

19. If 36,000 joules of work produce 5 amperes of current between two points for 60 seconds, what is the difference of potential between the two points, in volts?

   A. 600   B. 400   C. 120   D. 100

20. To measure a circuit current of 300 amps with a 100 amp ammeter, the shunt MUST have a MINIMUM capacity of _____ amps.

   A. 100   B. 200   C. 300   D. 400

21. A D.C. motor field coil connected first across a D.C. line and then across an A.C. line of equal voltage, will draw

   A. more current on D.C. than A.C.
   B. less current on D.C. than A.C.
   C. the same current on D.C. as on A.C.
   D. no current on A.C.

22. The single phase A.C. motor that produces the WEAKEST starting torque is the

   A. series A.C. motor   B. repulsion motor
   C. split phase motor   D. shaded pole motor

23. The D.C. generator whose terminal voltage falls off MOST rapidly when loaded is the _____ type.

   A. shunt   B. flat-compounded
   C. over-compounded   D. series

24. The E.M.F. produced by a primary cell depends on the

   A. size of the elements   B. amount of electrolyte
   C. distance between the elements
   D. materials used for the elements

25. A D.C. circuit consisting of 5 lamps in parallel draws 5 amperes; the current in *each* lamp is

   A. 1 ampere   B. 5 amperes
   C. determined by the resistance of the lamp
   D. 1/5 of an ampere

KEY (CORRECT ANSWERS)

1.	B	11.	D
2.	C	12.	B
3.	B	13.	A
4.	A	14.	B
5.	C	15.	A
6.	B	16.	C
7.	C	17.	A
8.	D	18.	C
9.	C	19.	C
10.	B	20.	B

21. A
22. D
23. A
24. D
25. C

TEST 3

DIRECTIONS: Each question or incomplete statement is followed by several suggested answers or completions. Select the one that BEST answers the question or completes the statement. *PRINT THE LETTER OF THE CORRECT ANSWER IN THE SPACE AT THE RIGHT.*

1. It is good practice to install a polarity reversing switch on a direct current fluorescent circuit to

   A. lessen ends blackening
   B. prevent one end from becoming dim
   C. ease starting
   D. prevent radio interference

   1.____

2. A 40-watt fluorescent lamp with necessary equipment may be satisfactorily operated from a direct current source of

   A. 110 volts   B. 220 volts
   C. either voltage   D. corrected power factor

   2.____

3. The National Electric Code provides that residential apartments be provided with receptacle outlets for *every* _____ feet of lineal wall space.

   A. 10   B. 15   C. 20   D. 25

   3.____

4. If a person is rendered unconscious by an electric shock, one should break the electrical contact, call a physician, *and*

   A. make patient comfortable until physician arrives
   B. use prone-pressure method of resuscitation
   C. administer a stimulant
   D. rub patient's body to increase circulation

   4.____

5. A 1 1/2" x 4" octagonal box may contain a MAXIMUM of

   A. 5 #14 conductors   B. 7 #14 conductors
   C. 8 #14 conductors   D. 11 #14 conductors

   5.____

6. A 1 1/2" x 4" square box may contain a MAXIMUM of

   A. 5 #14 conductors   B. 7 #14 conductors
   C. 8 #14 conductors   D. 11 #14 conductors

   6.____

7. Damaged cords for power tools should be

   A. coated with flux and covered with rubber tape
   B. repaired with insulating tape
   C. replaced
   D. shortened to remove the damaged section

   7.____

8. A source of direct current connected to a vibrating bell in series with the primary of an induction coil, will cause the secondary coil to produce

   A. alternating current
   B. direct current
   C. pulsating direct current
   D. interrupted direct current

9. Switches and attachment plugs installed in garages shall be AT LEAST _____ above the floor.

   A. 1 foot   B. 2 feet   C. 3 feet, 6 inches   D. 4 feet

10. Rigid conduit used for electrical wiring is purchased in

    A. 10 feet lengths, including coupling
    B. 10 feet lengths
    C. 9'6" lengths
    D. no standard lengths

11. Switches controlling signs shall be placed

    A. at the service equipment
    B. in the office of the premises displaying the sign
    C. within sight of the sign
    D. at the main entrance to the building

12. A self-excited alternator has

    A. slip rings for the field excitation
    B. a storage battery for the field
    C. a winding connected to the commutator
    D. no coil for direct current

13. A copper wire twice the diameter of another has a carrying capacity of _____ as great.

    A. two times   B. one-half   C. four times   D. eight times

14. The resistance of a copper bus bar is

    A. directly proportional to its length
    B. inversely proportional to its length
    C. negligible
    D. higher than that of gold

15. The resistance of a conductor depends upon the material it is made of and

    A. its temperature
    B. where it is used
    C. the ambient temperature
    D. method of installation

16. The positive terminal of an unmarked lead storage battery can *often* be identified by

    A. being larger than the negative
    B. being smaller than the negative
    C. removing the filling caps and looking at the plates
    D. using a "Y" box

17. The discharge voltage of an Edison storage cell is _____ volt(s).   17._____

    A. 1 B. 1.2 C. 2 D. 6

18. Voltmeters *often* have   18._____

    A. external shunts in parallel
    B. internal shunts
    C. internal resistance coils
    D. low resistance shunts

19. Selsyn motors are used   19._____

    A. to operate clocks from a direct current source
    B. at repeater stations
    C. as a generator for cathode ray tubes
    D. to charge storage batteries

20. The secondary of a current transformer   20._____

    A. is always opened with a connected load
    B. is never used with meters
    C. cannot be used on alternating current
    D. should never be opened while primary is energized

21. Circline is a development in   21._____

    A. fluorescent lighting
    B. raceways
    C. incandescent lighting
    D. insulating material

22. Neon signs operate on   22._____

    A. low voltage-high current
    B. high current-high voltage
    C. high voltage-low current
    D. low voltage-low current

23. Thermo electricity can be generated by heat applied to   23._____

    A. glass between two layers of aluminum foil
    B. two dissimilar metals
    C. two similar metals
    D. two lead plates in an electrolyte

24. To determine the power in a two-phase lighting and power system, the proper formula to use would be: 24._____

    A. $KW = \dfrac{E \times I \times PF}{1000}$
    B. $KW = 1.73 \times E \times I \times PF \times 1000$
    C. $KW = \dfrac{\sqrt{2} \times E \times I \times PF}{1000}$
    D. $KW = \dfrac{1.42 \times E \times W \times PF}{1000}$

25. An electric toaster operating on 120 volts has a resistance (hot) of 15 ohms. The wattage of the toaster is   25._____

    A. 1200 B. 1140 C. 1080 D. 960

KEY (CORRECT ANSWERS)

1.	B	11.	C
2.	B	12.	C
3.	C	13.	C
4.	B	14.	A
5.	C	15.	A
6.	C	16.	A
7.	C	17.	B
8.	A	18.	C
9.	D	19.	B
10.	A	20.	D

21. A
22. C
23. B
24. C
25. D

TEST 4

DIRECTIONS: Each question or incomplete statement is followed by several suggested answers or completions. Select the one that BEST answers the question or completes the statement. *PRINT THE LETTER OF THE CORRECT ANSWER IN THE SPACE AT THE RIGHT.*

1. When using lead cable, the inner radius of the bend shall be *no less than* _____ times the internal diameter of the conduit.   1._____

   A. four   B. six   C. eight   D. ten

2. A telephone hook switch is similar in operation to a   2._____

   A. strop key
   B. locking type push button
   C. locking type relay
   D. two circuit electrolier switch

3. The "dielectric" of a condenser is the   3._____

   A. air surrounding the condenser
   B. material separating the plates
   C. voltage impressed on the condenser
   D. lines of force established by the current

4. The depolarizing substance in the dry cell is   4._____

   A. manganese dioxide
   B. ammonium chloride
   C. zinc chloride
   D. lead oxide

5. The SMALLEST wattage fluorescent lamp manufactured for home use is   5._____

   A. 6   B. 8   C. 9   D. 15

6. The Carter system of connecting three-way switches for lighting   6._____

   A. will not operate lamps in parallel
   B. is not permitted under the National Electric Code
   C. will not operate when used in conjunction with a pilot light
   D. will not operate lamps in series

7. The material offering the LEAST resistance to the flow of an electric current is   7._____

   A. iron   B. aluminum   C. German silver   D. zinc

8. To replace a four-way switch, we may use the following type: 8._____

   A. Double pole snap
   B. Double pole, double throw
   C. Three-circuit electrolier
   D. Three-way switch

9. The LARGEST size conductor permitted in surface metal raceways is No.   9._____

   A. 10   B. 8   C. 6   D. 4

10. The energy accumulated in a storage battery is   10._____

    A. electrical   B. chemical   C. kinetic   D. mechanical

11. A strop key is MOST similar in operation to the following switch:

    A. Double pole
    B. Three-way
    C. Four-way
    D. Two circuit electrolier

12. Compensators are used to start motors at

    A. reduced voltage
    B. reduced speed
    C. reduced load
    D. increased voltage

13. A self-excited D.C. shunt generator is operating properly in clockwise rotation. If the direction of rotation is reversed, the

    A. brush polarity will reverse
    B. field polarity will reverse
    C. generator will fail to build up voltage
    D. output voltage will be the same in magnitude

14. If the intake port on an oil burner blower were closed, the motor would

    A. slow down
    B. require more current
    C. heat up
    D. require less current

15. In the event of a burnout of one single-phase transformer on a 3-phase, Wye-connected system, you can

    A. connect the remaining two in "delta"
    B. connect the remaining two "Scott"
    C. connect the remaining two "Open Wye"
    D. not connect them to obtain 3-phase with same voltage

16. The short circuited coil imbedded in the pole face of an A.C. contactor is used to

    A. blow out the arc
    B. reduce residual magnetism
    C. close the contactor
    D. reduce noise and vibration

17. A motor that is built for plugging service

    A. has a built-in brake
    B. helps to compensate power factor
    C. may be connected in reverse from full speed forward
    D. has built-in reduction gears

18. Eleven #14 conductors are permitted in a 1" conduit

    A. in apartment house risers
    B. under all conditions
    C. at no time
    D. for conductors between a motor and its controller

19. The number of mogul sockets on a two-wire branch circuit shall NOT exceed

    A. 8   B. 7   C. 6   D. 5

20. A 1 1/2" x 3 1/4" octagonal box may contain a MAXIMUM of

    A. 5 #14 conductors
    B. 7 #14 conductors
    C. 8 #14 conductors
    D. 11 #14 conductors

21. The average value of an alternating current is equal to its MAXIMUM value *times* 21.____
    A. 1.7232 B. .707 C. .636 D. 1.41

22. In a D.C. fire alarm system, the number of gongs allowed on a circuit is 22.____
    A. 10 B. 12 C. 13 D. 20

23. If the total resistance of the wire wound on a bipolar armature is 2 ohms, the armature resistance is _____ ohm(s). 23.____
    A. 1 B. 2 C. 1/2 D. 4

24. Increasing the field excitation of a synchronous motor will cause the 24.____
    A. motor to speed up
    B. motor to slow down
    C. current to lead
    D. voltage to lead

25. Mercury rectifiers have 25.____
    A. mercury anodes
    B. the positive terminal at the cathode
    C. high tank pressure
    D. one anode always

KEY (CORRECT ANSWERS)

1. D 11. B
2. A 12. A
3. B 13. C
4. A 14. C
5. A 15. C

6. B 16. B
7. B 17. C
8. B 18. D
9. C 19. B
10. B 20. C

21. C
22. C
23. C
24. B
25. C

EXAMINATION SECTION
TEST 1

DIRECTIONS: Each question or incomplete statement is followed by several suggested answers or completions. Select the one that *BEST* answers the question or completes the statement. *PRINT THE LETTER OF THE CORRECT ANSWER IN THE SPACE AT THE RIGHT.*

1. Employees of the transit system are cautioned, as a safety measure, not to use water to extinguish fires involving electrical equipment. One logical reason for this caution is that the water

    A. may transmit electrical shock to the user
    B. may crack hot insulation
    C. will not extinguish a fire started by electricity
    D. will cause harmful steam

2. As compared with solid wire, stranded wire of the same gage size is

    A. given a higher current rating
    B. easier to skin
    C. larger in total diameter
    D. better for high voltage

3. When drilling holes in concrete from the top of an extension ladder, it is *LEAST* important to

    A. wear goggles
    B. wear gloves
    C. hook one leg through the rung of the ladder
    D. wear a helmet

4. Motor frames are usually positively grounded by a special connection in order to

    A. remove static
    B. protect against lightning
    C. provide a neutral
    D. protect against shock

5. If a live conductor is contacted accidentally, the severity of the electrical shock is determined primarily by

    A. the size of the conductor
    B. whether the current is a.c. or d.c.
    C. the contact resistance
    D. the current in the conductor

Items 6-15.

Items 6 through 15 in Column I are electrical equipment parts each of which is commonly made from one of the materials listed in Column II. For each part in Column I, select the most appropriate material from Column II. *PRINT*, in the correspondingly numbered item space at the right, the letter given beside your selected material.

2 (#1)

COLUMN I	COLUMN II	
(electrical equipment parts)	(materials)	

6. d.c. circuit breaker arcing-tips   A. copper   6._____
7. cartridge fuse casing   B. silver   7._____
8. pig-tail jumpers for contacts   C. porcelain   8._____
9. commutator bars   D. carbon   9._____
10. bearing oil-rings   E. transite   10._____
11. cores for wound heater-coils   H. wood   11._____
12. center contact in screw lamp-sockets J. lead   12._____
13. acid storage battery terminals   K. brass   13._____
14. arc chutes   L. phosphor bronze 14._____
15. operating sticks for disconnecting   M. fiber   15._____
    switches

16. One of the rules of the transit system prohibits "horseplay". For electrical employees, this   16._____
    rule is most important because

    A. horseplay wastes company time
    B. electrical work does not permit relaxation at any time
    C. electrical work is very complicated
    D. men are liable to injury when so engaged

17. If a snap switch rated at 5 amperes is used for an electric heater which draws 10   17._____
    amperes, the most likely result is that the

    A. circuit fuse will be blown
    B. circuit wiring will become hot
    C. heater output will be halved
    D. switch contacts will become hot

18. If you are assigned by your foreman to a job which you do not understand, you should   18._____

    A. explain and request further instructions from your foreman
    B. try to do the job because you learn from experience
    C. do the job to the best of your ability as that is all that can be expected
    D. ask another foreman since your foreman should have explained the job when it
       was assigned

19. In carrying a length of conduit through a reasonably crowded subway station, a main-   19._____
    tainer and his helper would follow the best procedure if

    A. the helper held one end and the maintainer the other at arm's length downward
    B. the helper carried it near the middle and the maintainer went ahead to warn pas-
       sengers

C. each employee carried one end on his shoulder
D. the two employees carry at the 1/3 and 2/3 points respectively

20. To straighten a long length of wire, which has been tightly coiled, before pulling it into a conduit run, a good method is to

   A. roll the wire into a coil in the opposite direction
   B. fasten one end to the floor and whip it against the floor from the other end
   C. draw it over a convenient edge
   D. hold the wire at one end and twist it with the pliers from the other end

21. The 110-volt bus supplying the control power in a substation is often d.c. from storage batteries charged automatically rather than a.c. from a transformer using the a.c. main supply. One reason is that the d.c. system

   A. requires less maintenance
   B. is more reliable
   C. requires less power
   D. permits smaller control wires

22. Mercury arc rectifiers are often used rather than rotary converters in above-ground substations in residential areas because they are

   A. cooler   B. less dangerous
   C. smaller   D. less noisy

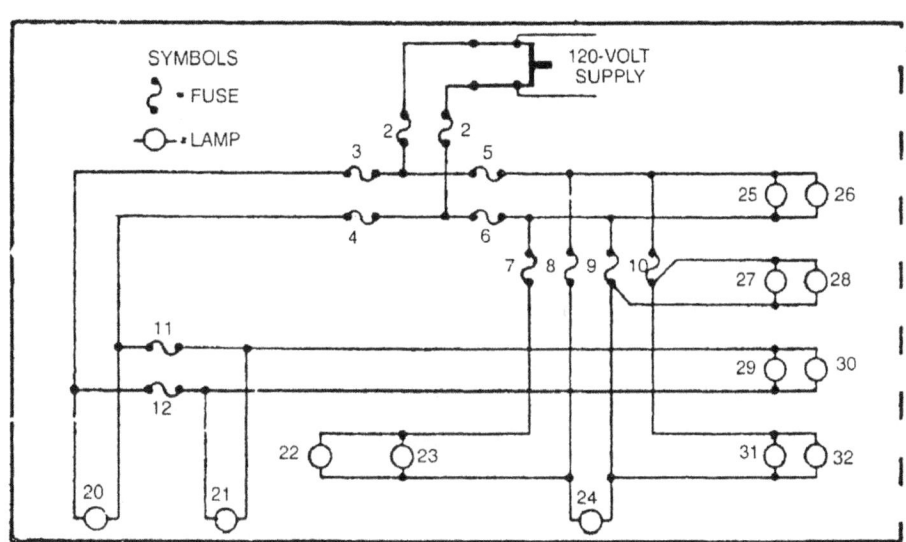

Items 23 - 31.

Items 23 through 31 are based on the above wiring diagram. All of the lamps are normally lighted. These items in Column I are descriptions of abnormal conditions each of which is caused by one of the faults listed in Column II. *PRINT*, in the correspondingly numbered item space at the right, the letter given beside your selected fault.

	Column I (abnormal conditions)		Column II (faults)	
23.	Lamp Nos. 24, 27, 28, 31, and 32 dark	A.	Either fuse #11 or fuse #12 blown	23.____
24.	Lamp Nos. 27, 28, 31, and 32 dark	B.	Fuse #9 blown	24.____
25.	Lamp Nos. 21, 29, and 30 dark	C.	Fuse #10 blown	25.____
26.	Lamp Nos. 22 and 23 dark	D.	Lamp burned out	26.____
27.	Only lamp No. 24 dark	E.	Either fuse #9 or fuse #10 blown	27.____
28.	Lamp Nos. 20, 21, 29, and 30 dark	H.	Either fuse #5 or fuse #6 blown	28.____
29.	Lamp Nos. 22, 23, and 24 dark	J.	Fuse #8 blown	29.____
		K.	Fuse #7 blown	
30.	Lamp Nos. 22, 23, 24, 25, 26, 27, 28, 31, and 32 dark	L.	Either fuse #3 or fuse #4 blown	30.____
31.	Only lamp No. 20 dark			31.____
		M.	Either fuse #1 or fuse #2 blown	

32. The wire size most commonly used for branch circuits in residences is 32.____

    A. #14   B. #16   C. #12   D. #18

33. If the applied voltage on an incandescent lamp is increased 10%, the lamp will 33.____

    A. have a longer life
    B. consume less power
    C. burn more brightly
    D. fail by insulation breakdown

34. You would expect that the overload trip coil on an ordinary air circuit breaker would have 34.____

    A. heavy wire   B. fine wire
    C. many turns   D. heavily insulated wire

35. A cycle counter is an electrical timer which, when energized by alternating current, counts the number of cycles until it is deenergized. If a cycle counter is energized from a 60-cycle power supply for ten seconds, the reading of the instrument should be 35.____

    A. 6   B. 10   C. 60   D. 600

36. Artificial respiration should be administered to the victim of electric shock ONLY if he is NOT 36.____

    A. conscious   B. bleeding
    C. breathing   D. burned

37. A rule of the transit system states that, "In walking on the track, walk opposite the direction of traffic on that track if possible". By logical reasoning, the principal safety idea behind this rule is that the man on the track

    A. is more likely to see an approaching train
    B. will be seen more readily by the motorman
    C. need not be as careful
    D. is better able to judge the speed of the train

37._____

38. The most practical way to determine in the field if a large coil of #14 wire has the required length for a given job is to

    A. weigh the coil
    B. measure one turn and count the turns
    C. unroll it into another coil
    D. make a visual comparison with a full coil

38._____

39. A frequency meter is constructed as a potential device, that is, to be connected across the line. A logical reason for this is that

    A. only the line voltage has frequency
    B. a transformer may then be used with it
    C. the reading will be independent of the varying current
    D. it is safer than a series device

39._____

40. If you feel that one of your co-workers is not doing his share of the work, your best procedure is to

    A. point this out to the foreman
    B. reduce your output to bring the matter to a head
    C. increase your own output as a good example
    D. take no action and continue to do your job properly

40._____

41. It is usually not safe to connect 110 volts d.c. to a magnet coil designed for 110 volts a.c. because the

    A. insulation is insufficient
    B. iron may overheat
    C. wire may overheat
    D. inductance may be too high

41._____

42. The most satisfactory temporary replacement for a 40-watt, 120-volt incandescent lamp, if an identical replacement is not available, is a lamp rated at

    A. 100 watts, 240 volts
    B. 60 watts, 130 volts
    C. 40 watts, 32 volts
    D. 15 watts, 120 volts

42._____

43. If the following bare copper wire sizes were arranged in the order of increasing weight per 1000 feet, the correct arrangement would be

    A. #00, #40, #8
    B. #40, #00, #8
    C. #00, #8, #40
    D. #40, #8, #00

43._____

44. The purpose of having a rheostat in the field circuit of a d.c. shunt motor is to

   A. control the speed of the motor
   B. minimize the starting current
   C. limit the field current to a safe value
   D. reduce sparking at the brushes

45. If the maintainer to whom you are assigned gives you a job to be done in a certain way and, after starting the job, you think of another method which you are convinced is better, you should

   A. follow the procedure given by the maintainer since he most likely would insist on his method anyhow
   B. request his opinion of your method before proceeding further
   C. try your own method since the maintainer probably will not know the difference
   D. inform the foreman next time he comes around

46. The resistance of a 1000-ft. length of a certain size copper wire is required to be 10.0 ohms $\pm$ 2%. This wire would NOT be acceptable if the resistance was

   A. 10.12 ohms
   B. 10.02 ohms
   C. 10.22 ohms
   D. 9.82 ohms

47. The LEAST important action in making a good soldered connection between two wires is to

   A. use the proper flux
   B. clean the wires well
   C. use plenty of solder
   D. use sufficient heat

48. When you are newly assigned as a helper to an experienced maintainer, he is most likely to give you good training if your attitude is that

   A. he is responsible for your progress
   B. he should do the jobs where little is to be learned
   C. you need the benefit of his experience
   D. you have the basic knowledge but lack the details

49. According to the rules, electrical maintainers must not permit other employees to replace lamps of authorized wattage with lamps of higher wattage in the working areas of such employees. The most likely reason for this rule is

   A. to prevent such employees from injuring their eyes
   B. that higher wattage lamps cost more
   C. to avoid overloading lighting circuits
   D. to keep the cost of electricity down

50. In the subway system, it would be most logical to expect to find floodlights located in the

   A. under-river tunnels
   B. outdoor train storage yards
   C. section maintenance headquarters
   D. subway storage rooms

KEY (CORRECT ANSWERS)

1. A	11. C	21. B	31. D	41. C
2. C	12. L	22. D	32. A	42. B
3. D	13. J	23. B	33. C	43. D
4. D	14. E	24. C	34. A	44. A
5. C	15. H	25. A	35. D	45. B
6. D	16. D	26. K	36. C	46. C
7. M	17. D	27. D	37. A	47. C
8. A	18. A	28. L	38. B	48. C
9. A	19. A	29. J	39. C	49. C
10. K	20. B	30. H	40. D	50. B

TEST 2

DIRECTIONS: Each question or incomplete statement is followed by several suggested answers or completions. Select the one that BEST answers the question or completes the statement. *PRINT THE LETTER OF THE CORRECT ANSWER IN THE SPACE AT THE RIGHT.*

1. Of the following, the best conductor of electricity is   1.____

   A. tungsten   B. iron   C. aluminum   D. carbon

2. A 600-volt cartridge fuse is most readily distinguished from a 250-volt cartridge fuse of the same ampere rating by comparing the   2.____

   A. insulating materials used
   B. shape of the ends
   C. diameters
   D. lengths

3. When carrying conduit, employees are cautioned against lifting with the fingers inserted in the end. The probable reason for this caution is to avoid the possibility of   3.____

   A. dropping and damaging the conduit
   B. getting dirt or perspiration inside
   C. cutting the fingers on the edge of the conduit
   D. straining finger muscles

4. Many power-transformer cases are filled with oil. The purpose of the oil is to   4.____

   A. prevent rusting of the core
   B. reduce a-c hum
   C. insulate the coils from the case
   D. transmit heat from the coils and core case

5. In order to make certain that a 600 volt circuit is dead V. before working on it, the best procedure is to   5.____

   A. test with a voltmeter
   B. "short" the circuit quickly with a piece of insulated wire
   C. see if any of the insulated conductors are warm
   D. disconnect one of the wires of the circuit near the feed

6. Electrical maintainers in the transit system are generally instructed in first aid in case of electrical shock. The most likely reason for this procedure is to   6.____

   A. decrease the number of accidents
   B. provide temporary emergency aid
   C. eliminate the need for calling a doctor
   D. reduce the necessity for "killing" circuits for maintenance

7. When closing an exposed knife switch on a panel, the action should be positive and rapid because there is less likelihood of   7.____

   A. the operator receiving a shock
   B. the operator being burned

72

C. the fuse blowing
D. injury to equipment connected to the circuit

8. Lubrication is *NEVER* used on   8._____

   A. a knife switch
   B. a die when threading conduit
   C. wires being pulled into a conduit
   D. a commutator

9. If one plug fuse in a 110-volt circuit blows because of a short-circuit, a 110-volt lamp   9._____
   screwed into the fuse socket will

   A. burn dimly   B. remain dark
   C. burn out   D. burn normally

10. Of the following, the *LEAST* undesirable practice if a specified wire size is not available   10._____
    for part of a circuit is to

    A. use two wires of 1/2 capacity in parallel as a substitute
    B. use the next larger size wire
    C. use a smaller size wire if the length is short
    D. reduce the size of the fuse and use smaller wire

11. If it is necessary to increase slightly the tension of an ordinary coiled spring in a relay, the   11._____
    proper procedure is to

    A. cut off one or two turns
    B. compress it slightly
    C. stretch it slightly
    D. unhook one end, twist and replace

12. The most important reason for insisting on neatness in maintenance quarters is that it   12._____

    A. makes a good impression on visitors and officials
    B. decreases the chances of accidents to employees
    C. provides jobs to fill the unavoidable gaps in daily routine
    D. prevents tools from becoming rusty

Items 13-21.

Items 13 through 21 in Column I are wiring devices each of which properly would be used at one of the locations indicated by a large dot (●) on one of the four sketches shown in Column II. For each device in Column I, select the suitable location from Column II. *PRINT,* in the correspondingly numbered item space at the right, the letter given beside your selected location.

3 (#2)

COLUMN I	COLUMN II	
ITEM		
13.		13. ____
14.		14. ____
15.		15. ____
16.		16. ____
17.		17. ____
18.		18. ____
19.		19. ____
20.		20. ____
21.		21. ____

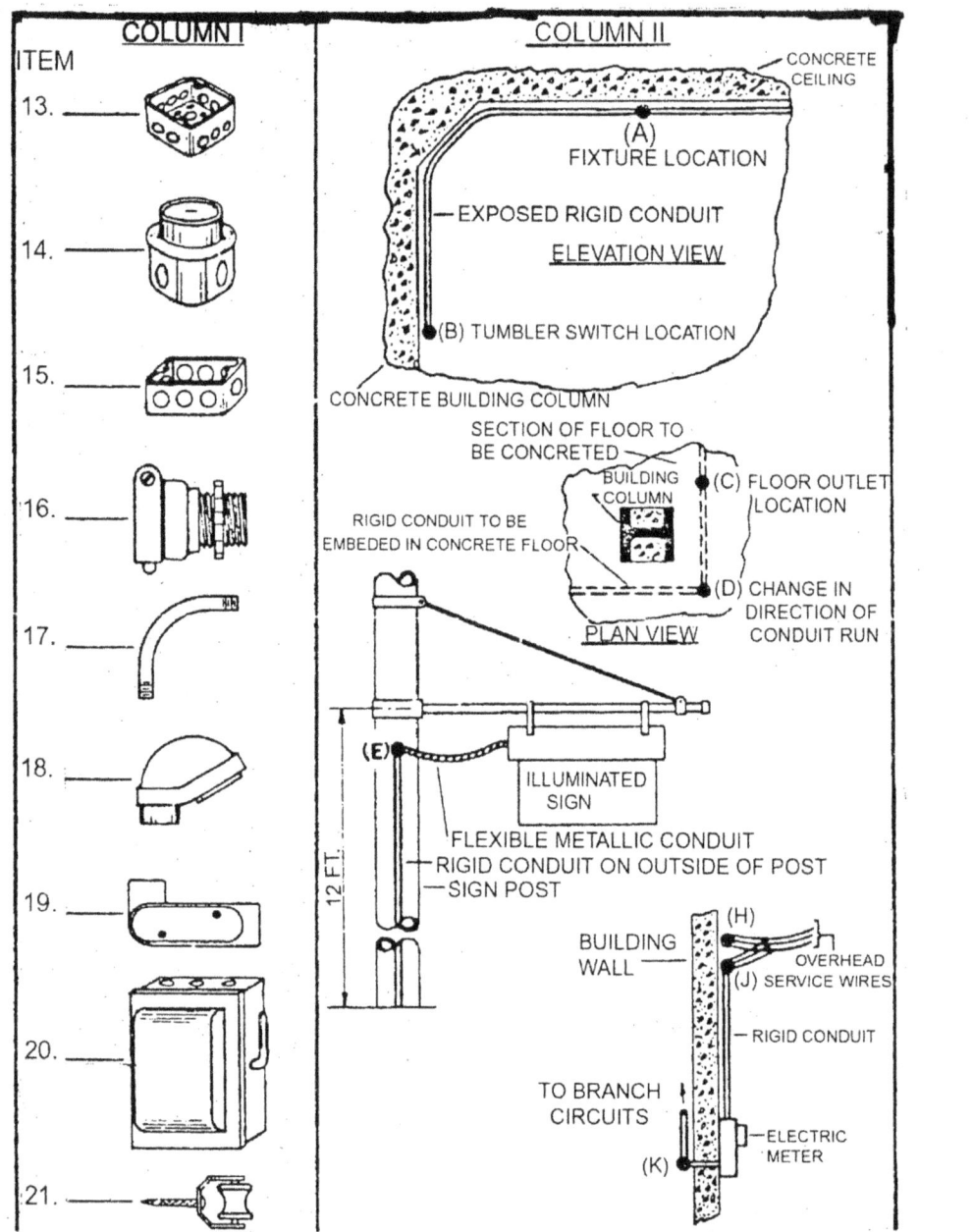

74

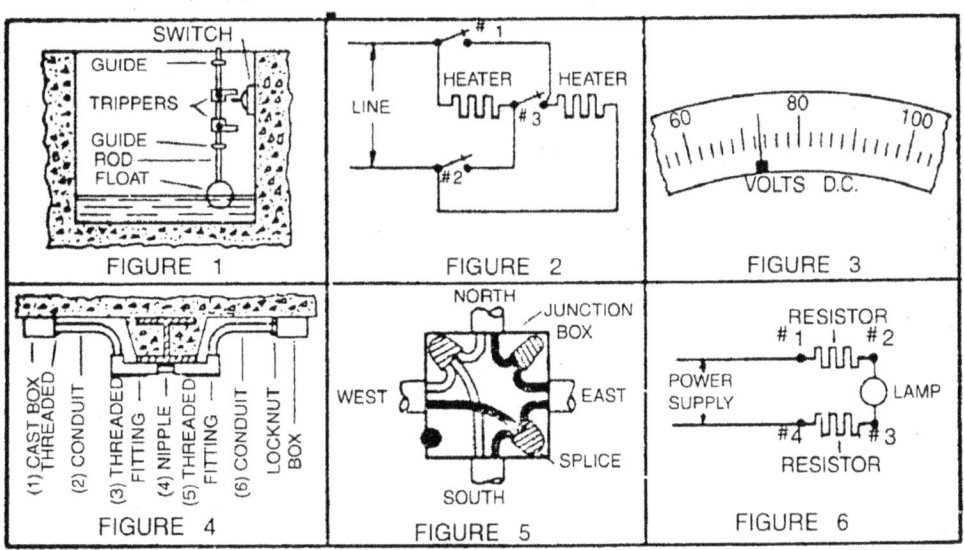

Items 22 - 27.

Items 22 through 27 refer to the figures above. Each item gives the proper figure to use with that item.

22. In Figure 1, the trippers on the float-rod operate the switch and are adjusted to start the pump motor when the water in the sump reaches a certain high level and to stop the pump when the water is down to a certain low level.
    If it is decided that the pump should start sooner, the required change in tripper position on the rod is

    A. upper tripper lowered
    B. lower tripper lowered
    C. upper tripper raised
    D. lower tripper raised

    22.____

23. In Figure 2, the greatest total amount of heat will be provided by the two heaters if

    A. switches #2 and #3 are closed
    B. switch #3 is closed
    C. switches #1 and #3 are closed
    D. switches #1, #2 and #3 are closed

    23.____

24. The voltage indicated on the voltmeter scale of Figure 3 is

    A. 73.0   B. 71.5   C. 66.5   D. 60.65

    24.____

25. In Figure 4, if fitting (3) is defective and must be replaced, the proper sequence of disassembly is to remove in the order given

    A. 2 then 3
    B. 4 then 3
    C. 1, 2 and 3 together; then 3
    D. 6 and 5 together; then 4 and 3

    25.____

26. If the wiring in the junction box of Figure 5 is in accord with recognized good wiring practice, the power supply wires could NOT be those in the conduit going

    A. north   B. south   C. east   D. west

    26.____

27. The lamp of Figure 6 is at normal brightness connected as shown. Using a third resistor, the greatest reduction in lamp brightness occurs if that resistor is connected between points

    A. #1 and #4   B. #1 and #2
    C. #2 and #3   D. #3 and #4

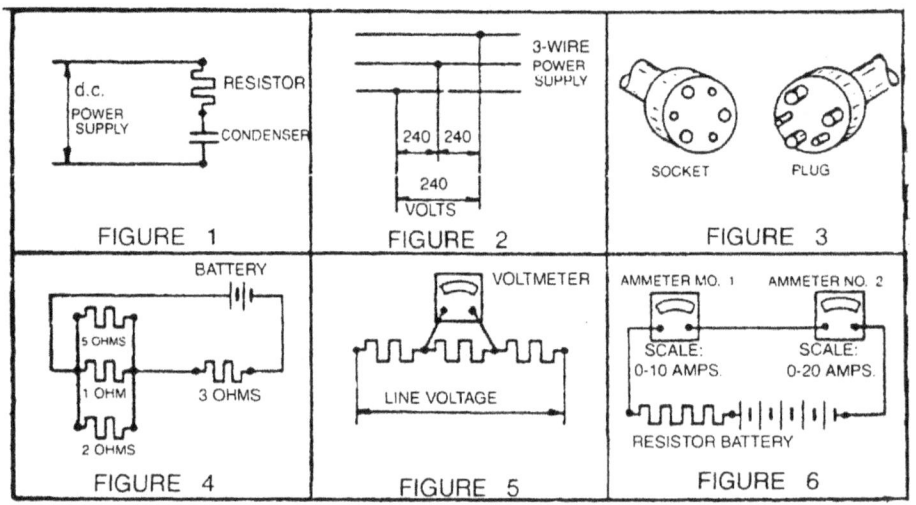

Items 28 - 33.

Items 28 through 33 refer to the figures above. Each item gives the proper figure to use with that item.

28. In Figure 1, if the voltage of the power supply is constant, the voltage across the condenser is

    A. zero
    B. variable
    C. equal to the supply voltage
    D. more than the supply voltage

29. In accordance with the voltages shown in Figure 2, the power supply must be

    A. single-phase a.c.   B. two-phase a.c.
    C. three-phase a.c.   D. three-wire d.c.

30. With respect to the plug and socket in Figure 3, it is clear that the plug

    A. cannot be inserted into the socket
    B. can be inserted into the socket only one way
    C. can be inserted only two ways into the socket
    D. can be inserted three ways into the socket

31. Without knowing the battery voltage in Figure 4, it is clear that the highest current is in the

    A. 5-ohm resistor   B. 3-ohm resistor
    C. 2-ohm resistor   D. 1-ohm resistor

32. If the three resistors in Figure 5 are of equal and relatively low resistance, the voltmeter should read

    A. one-third line voltage
    B. one-half line voltage
    C. two-thirds line voltage
    D. full line voltage

33. If the current in the circuit of Figure 6 is 6 amperes, the ammeters should read

    A. 4 amp. on meter #1 and 2 amp. on meter #2
    B. 6 amp. on each meter
    C. 2 amp. on meter #1 and 4 amp. on meter #2
    D. 3 amp. on each meter

34. The voltage drop is 24 volts across resistor

    A. #1   B. #2
    C. #3   D. #4

35. If ammeter #2 reads 60 amp., the reading of ammeter #1 should be about
    A. 4 amp.
    B. 15 amp.
    C. 60 amp.
    D. 900 amp.

36. If fuse #1 blows in the 3-wire d.c. system shown, the current in the neutral wire will
    A. increase by 1.0 amp.
    B. increase by 0.5 amp.
    C. decrease by 1.0 amp.
    D. decrease by 0.5 amp.

37. The current in the 4-ohm resistor is
    A. 5 amp.
    B. 4 amp.
    C. 3 amp.
    D. 1 amp.

38. On the transformer, the dimension marked "X" is
    A. 9 7/8"
    B. 14"
    C. 18 1/8"
    D. 19 1/8"

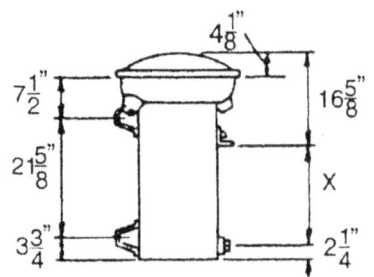

39. With the voltage drop across the four resistors as shown, the voltmeter will read
    A. 50 volts
    B. 70 volts
    C. 100 volts
    D. 170 volts

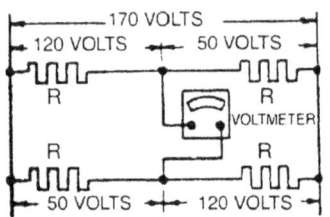

40. If each circuit originates at the switchboard, the total amount of wire required for the conduit runs shown (neglecting connections) is
    A. 5300 ft.
    B. 2650 ft.
    C. 2400 ft.
    D. 1600 ft.

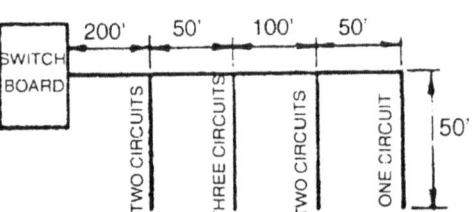

NOTE: TWO WIRES PER CIRCUIT

41. If the permissible current is 1,000 amperes for each square inch of cross section, the bus bar shown can carry
    A. 2250 amp.
    B. 2000 amp.
    C. 1750 amp.
    D. 1500 amp.

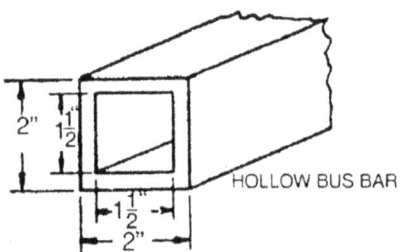

42. If the slider connecting both resistors is 9 inches from the left-hand end of the resistors, the resistance between terminals #1 and #2 is
    A. 1125 ohms
    B. 875 ohms
    C. 750 ohms
    D. 625 ohms

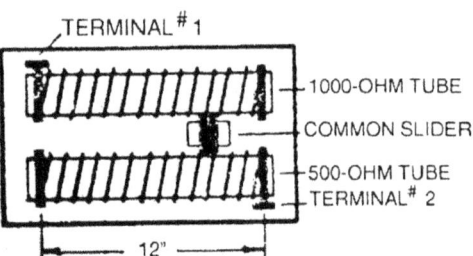

43. If the voltmeter reads 80 volts, the current in the 11-ohm resistor is
    A. 10 amp.
    B. 6.3 amp.
    C. 12 amp.
    D. 8.3 amp.

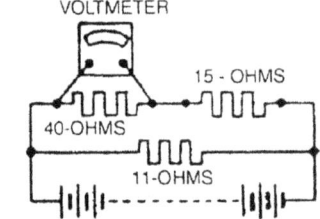

Questions 44 - 50.

Questions 44 through 50 show common electrical jobs. Each item shows four methods (A), (B), (C), and (D) of doing the particular job. Only ONE of the four methods is entirely CORRECT in accordance with good practice. For each item, examine the four sketches and select the sketch showing the correct method. PRINT, in the correspondingly numbered item space at the right, the letter given below your selected sketch.

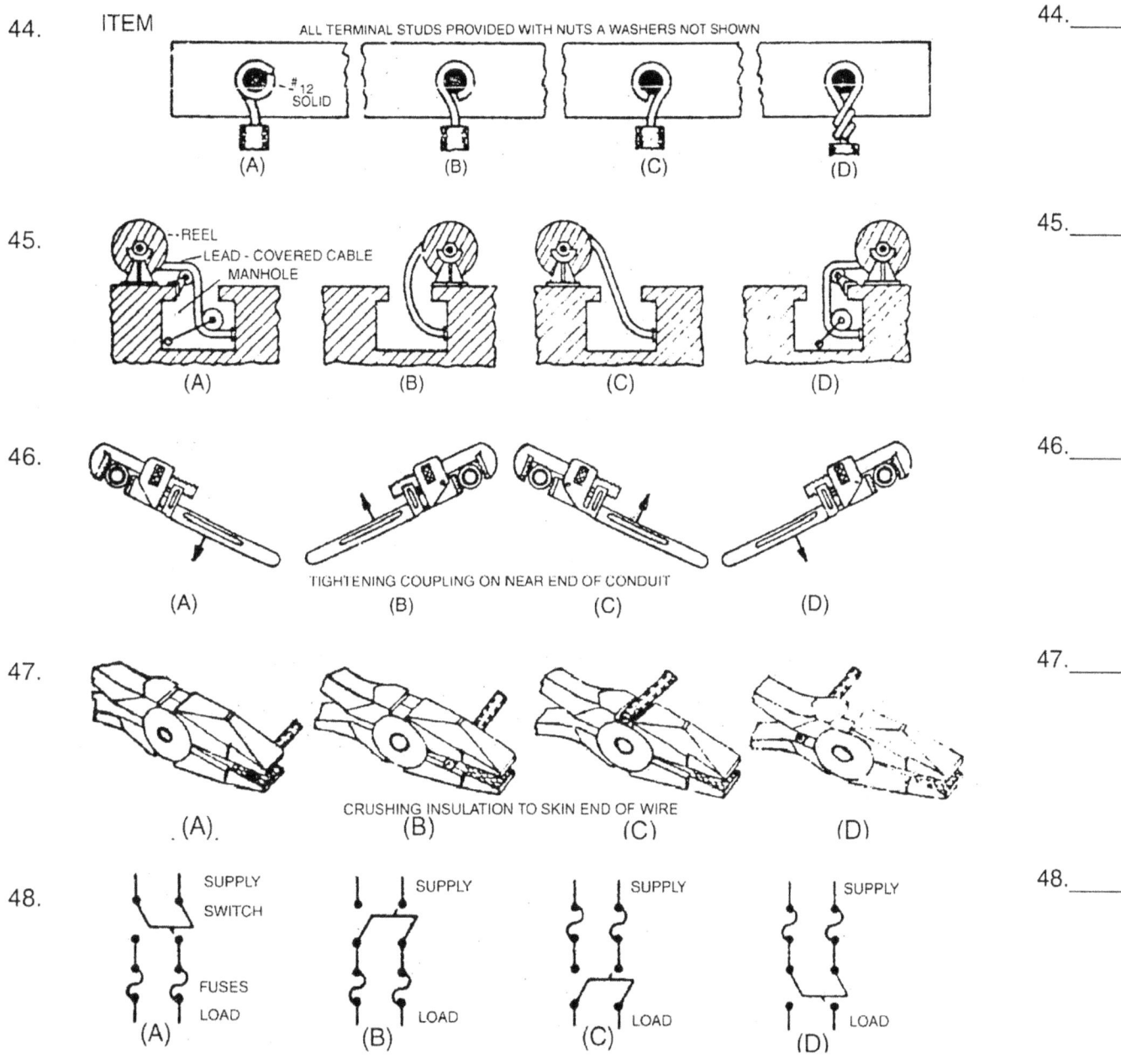

44. _____

45. _____

46. _____

47. _____

48. _____

9 (#2)

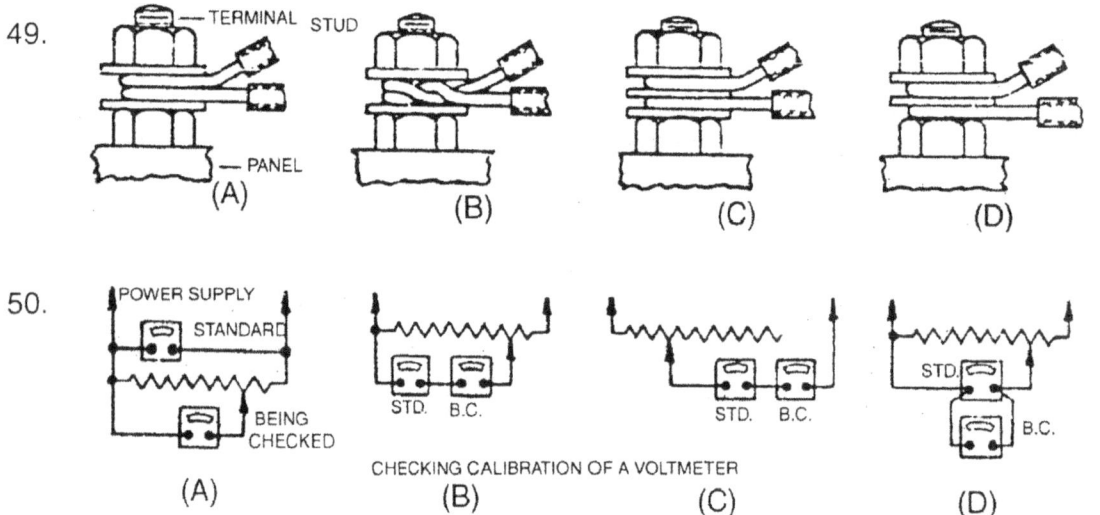

49.
49.

50.
50.

CHECKING CALIBRATION OF A VOLTMETER

KEY (CORRECT ANSWERS)

1. C	11. A	21. H	31. B	41. C
2. D	12. B	22. D	32. A	42. B
3. C	13. A	23. C	33. B	43. A
4. D	14. C	24. A	34. A	44. B
5. A	15. B	25. D	35. A	45. B
6. B	16. E	26. C	36. B	46. A
7. B	17. D	27. C	37. C	47. D
8. D	18. J	28. C	38. C	48. B
9. D	19. E	29. C	39. B	49. C
10. B	20. K	30. D	40. A	50. D

EXAMINATION SECTION
TEST 1

DIRECTIONS: Each question or incomplete statement is followed by several suggested answers or completions. Select the one that BEST answers the question or completes the statement. *PRINT THE LETTER OF THE CORRECT ANSWER IN THE SPACE AT THE RIGHT.*

1. Motor speeds are *generally* measured directly in RPM by the use of a

    A. potentiometer
    B. manometer
    C. dynamometer
    D. tachometer

2. Asbestos is used as a wire covering *mainly* for protection against

    A. humidity   B. vibration   C. corrosion   D. heat

3. Assume that you were asked to get the tools for a maintainer to use in taking down a run of exposed conduit (including outlet boxes) from its installed location on the surface of a concrete wall. The combination of tools which would *probably* prove MOST useful would be

    A. Stillson wrenches, a box wrench, and a hacksaw
    B. hacksaw, a screw driver, and an adjustable open-end wrench
    C. screw driver, a hammer, and a box wrench
    D. screw driver, an adjustable open-end wrench, and Stillson wrenches

4. Locknuts are frequently used in making electrical connections on terminal boards. The purpose of the locknuts is to

    A. eliminate the use of flat washers
    B. prevent unauthorized personnel from tampering with the connections
    C. keep the connections from loosening through vibration
    D. increase the contact area at the connection point

5. The fasteners used to mount a cast iron box on a hollow tile wall are

    A. machine screws
    B. lag screws
    C. toggle bolts
    D. steel cut nails

6. The *primary* purpose of galvanizing steel conduit is to

    A. increase mechanical strength
    B. retard rusting
    C. provide a good surface for painting
    D. provide good electrical contact for grounding

7. The BEST immediate first aid if electrolyte splashes into the eyes when filling a storage battery is to

    A. bandage the eyes to keep out light
    B. wipe the eyes dry with a soft towel
    C. induce tears to flow by staring at a bright light
    D. bathe the eyes with plenty of clean water

8. Transit workers are advised to report injuries caused by nails, no matter how slight. The MOST important reason for this rule is that this type of injury

   A. is caused by violating safety rules
   B. can only be caused by carelessness
   C. generally causes dangerous bleeding
   D. may result in a serious condition

9. The MOST important reason for using a fuse-puller when removing a cartridge fuse from the fuse clips is to

   A. prevent blowing of the fuse
   B. prevent injury to the fuse element
   C. reduce the chances of personal injury
   D. reduce arcing at the fuse clips

10. The *three* elements of a transistor are

    A. collector, base, emitter
    B. collector, grid, cathode
    C. plate, grid, emitter
    D. plate, base, cathode

11. The abbreviation D.P.D.T. used in electrical work describes a type of

    A. switch   B. motor   C. fuse   D. generator

12. The device used to change a.c. to d.c. is a

    A. frequency changer
    B. regulator
    C. transformer
    D. rectifier

13. The core of an electro-magnet is *usually* made of

    A. lead   B. iron   C. brass   D. aluminium

14. The application of lubricating oil to parts of electrical contacts is *generally* considered POOR practice.
    The MAIN reason for this is that the

    A. contacts will slip too much
    B. oil would cause poor electrical contact
    C. oil would reduce the contact resistance
    D. oil would cause a fire

15. Nichrome wire would be MOST suitable for use in

    A. a transformer
    B. a motor
    C. a heating element
    D. an incandescent lamp

16. To smooth out the ripples present in rectified a.c., the device *commonly* used is a

    A. filter   B. relay   C. spark gap   D. booster

17. One DISADVANTAGE of porcelain as an insulator is that it is

    A. only good for low voltage
    B. not satisfactory on a.c. circuits
    C. a brittle material
    D. difficult to clean

18. The gage used to determine the size of wire is called   18.____

    A. AWG   B. NPT   C. PILC   D. RHW

19. A stranded wire is given the same size designation as a solid wire if it has the same   19.____

    A. cross-sectional area   B. weight per foot
    C. overall diameter   D. strength

20. The normal voltage of the electrical circuits in most homes and offices in this area is 120. The *difference* between the maximum power that can be supplied by a 20-ampere circuit and the maximum that can be supplied by a 15-ampere circuit is   20.____

    A. 4200 watts   B. 2400 watts   C. 1800 watts   D. 600 watts

21. The term which is NOT applicable in describing the construction of a microphone is   21.____

    A. dynamic   B. carbon   C. crystal   D. feedback

22. The magnetic material used in making the high-strength permanent magnets which are now readily available, is *commonly* known as   22.____

    A. alnico   B. chromaloy   C. nichrome   D. advance

23. If a two wire circuit has a drop of 2 volts in each wire to the load and a supply voltage of 100 volts, the voltage at the load is _____ volts.   23.____

    A. 104   B. 102   C. 98   D. 96

24. A milliampere is _____ amperes.   24.____

    A. 1000   B. 100   C. .01   D. .001

25. A megohm is _____ ohms.   25.____

    A. 10   B. 100   C. 1000   D. 1,000,000

26. A circular mil is a measure of electrical conductor   26.____

    A. length   B. area   C. volume   D. weight

27. A standard pipe thread differs from a standard screw thread in that the pipe thread   27.____

    A. is tapered
    B. is deeper
    C. requires no lubrication when cutting
    D. has the same pitch for any diameter of pipe

28. The rating term "1000 ohms, 10 watts" would *generally* be applied to a   28.____

    A. heater   B. relay   C. resistor   D. transformer

29. The term "60 cycle" as applied to alternating current means   29.____

    A. one cycle in 60 seconds   B. 60 cycles per second
    C. 60 cycles per minute   D. one cycle in 60 minutes

30. The dimensions of the concrete base shown below are   30.____

    A. 12" x 20"   B. 19" x 25"   C. 21" x 27"   D. 24" x 29"

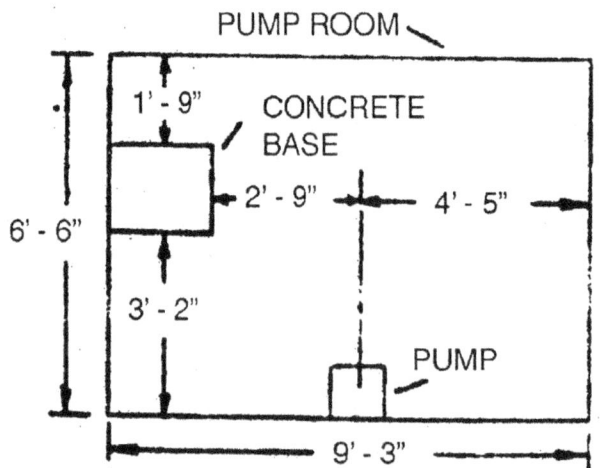

31. Two separate adjacent lamp bulbs are placed behind each colored lens of the train signals alongside the tracks in the subway.
   The *logical* reason why two bulbs are used instead of one bulb is to

   A. permit lower line voltage
   B. increase the light intensity
   C. permit the use of smaller bulbs
   D. keep the signal lighted in case one bulb fails

32. The action of a common plug fuse depends on the principle that the

   A. current develops heat
   B. voltage breaks down a thin mica disk
   C. current expands and bends a link
   D. voltage develops heat

33. The load side is *usually* wired to the blades of a knife switch to

   A. prevent arcing when switch is opened
   B. make the blades dead when switch is open
   C. allow changing of fuses without opening switch
   D. prevent blowing fuse when opening switch

34. Two 500-watt lamps connected in series across a 110-volt line draw 2 amperes.
    The *total* power consumed is _____ watts.

    A. 1,000   B. 250   C. 220   D. 55

35. Before connecting two generators in parallel to a common bus they should ALWAYS have the same

    A. voltage   B. capacity   C. resistance   D. speed

36. Certain electrical control circuits in power stations must be kept energized at all times even in case of complete station shut down.
    Based on this fact, the BEST source of power supply for these circuit is from

    A. the main generator   B. a motor-generator set
    C. a rectifier   D. a storage battery

37. Electrical helpers on the subway system are instructed in the use of fire extinguishers. The *probable* reason for including helpers in this instruction is that the helper

    A. cannot do the more important work
    B. may be the cause of a fire because of his inexperience
    C. may be alone when a fire starts
    D. will become interested in fire prevention

37.____

38. If a 100-watt tungsten lamp is compared with a 25-watt tungsten lamp of the same voltage rating, the resistance of the 100-watt lamp is

    A. higher
    B. lower
    C. the same
    D. higher with A.C., lower with D.C.

38.____

39. If a low resistance is connected in parallel with a higher resistance, the combined resistance is

    A. ALWAYS *less* than the low resistance
    B. ALWAYS *more* than the high resistance
    C. ALWAYS between the values of the high and the low resistance
    D. *higher* or *lower* than the low resistance depending on the value of the higher resistance

39.____

40. Connecting dry cells in parallel instead of in series

    A. *increases* the current capacity of the battery
    B. *decreases* the current capacity of the battery
    C. *increases* the battery voltage
    D. *decreases* the life of the battery

40.____

KEY (CORRECT ANSWERS)

1.	D	11.	A	21.	D	31.	D
2.	D	12.	D	22.	A	32.	A
3.	D	13.	B	23.	D	33.	B
4.	C	14.	B	24.	D	34.	C
5.	C	15.	C	25.	D	35.	A
6.	B	16.	A	26.	B	36.	D
7.	D	17.	C	27.	A	37.	C
8.	D	18.	A	28.	C	38.	B
9.	C	19.	A	29.	B	39.	A
10.	A	20.	D	30.	B	40.	A

TEST 2

DIRECTIONS: Each question or incomplete statement is followed by several suggested answers or completions. Select the one that BEST answers the question or completes the statement. *PRINT THE LETTER OF THE CORRECT ANSWER IN THE SPACE AT THE RIGHT.*

1. Maintainers of the transit system are required to report defective equipment to their superiors, even when the maintenance of the particular equipment is handled entirely by another bureau.
   The purpose of this rule is to

   A. fix responsibility
   B. discourage slackers
   C. encourage alertness
   D. prevent accidents

   1.____

2. To determine which wire of a two-wire 120-volt a.c. line is the underground wire, the BEST procedure is to

   A. obtain the polarity by connecting a voltmeter across the line
   B. quickly ground each line in turn
   C. connect one lead of a test lamp to the conduit; and test with the other
   D. test with the fingers to ground

   2.____

3. Condensers are often connected across relay contacts that make and break frequently. The purpose of using condensers in this manner is to

   A. store a charge for the next operation
   B. reduce pitting of the contacts
   C. balance the inductance of the circuit
   D. make the relay slow acting

   3.____

4. A conductor used as a ground wire is *usually*

   A. insulated
   B. clamped to the metallic ground
   C. fused
   D. #14 A.W.G.

   4.____

5. If fuse clips become hot under normal circuit load, the MOST probable cause is that the fuse

   A. rating is too low
   B. rating is too high
   C. clips are too loose
   D. clips are too tight

   5.____

6. The liquid in a lead-acid storage battery is called the

   A. anode
   B. cathode
   C. electrolyte
   D. electrode

   6.____

7. In carrying a length of conduit through a reasonably crowded subway station, a maintainer and his helper would follow the BEST procedure if

   A. the helper held one end and the maintainer the other at arm's length downward
   B. the helper carried it near the middle and the maintainer went ahead to warn passengers
   C. each employee carried one end on his shoulder
   D. the two employees carry at the 1/3 and 2/3 points respectively

   7.____

8. As a helper you are assigned to work with a maintainer. During the course of the work, you realize that the maintainer is about to violate a basic safety rule.
   In this case the BEST thing for you to do is to

   A. walk away from him so that you will not become involved
   B. say nothing until he actually violates this rule and then call it to his attention
   C. immediately call it to his attention
   D. say nothing, but later report this action to the foreman

9. A rule of the transit system is that the system telephones must NOT be used for personal calls.
   The MOST important reason for this rule is that such personal calls

   A. increase telephone maintenance
   B. tie up telephones which may be urgently needed for company business
   C. waste company time
   D. require additional operators

10. Commutators are found on

    A. mercury rectifiers
    B. D.C. motors
    C. circuit breakers
    D. alternators

11. A 200 R.P.M. motor has its centrifugal speed switch set to open at 110% speed.
    The switch will open at _____ R.P.M.

    A. 310
    B. 220
    C. 110
    D. 10

12. A 2-ohm resistor and a 1-ohm resistor connected in parallell2 take a total current of 30 amperes.
    The current in the 1-ohm resistor is _____ amperes.

    A. 10
    B. 15
    C. 20
    D. 30

13. The device *commonly* used to measure the insulation resistance of a transformer winding is

    A. an ammeter
    B. a megger
    C. a wattmeter
    D. a Wheatstone bridge

14. A D.C. wattmeter has

    A. a voltage coil and a current coil
    B. two current coils
    C. two voltage coils
    D. three current coils

15. A 10-24 machine screw necessarily differs from a 12-24 machine screw in

    A. diameter
    B. threads per inch
    C. length
    D. shape of head

16. A power transformer with a ratio of 2 to 1 is fully loaded with 1,000 watts on the secondary.
    It is reasonable to expect a primary input of _____ watts.

    A. 500
    B. 990
    C. 1010
    D. 2000

17. The helper who would probably be rated *highest* by his supervisor is the one who

    A. makes many suggestions on work procedures
    B. never lets the maintainer do heavy lifting
    C. asks many questions about the work
    D. listens to instructions and carries them out

18. A "shunt" is used in parallel with a meter measuring high currents to

    A. increase the meter resistance
    B. protect the meter against short circuits
    C. reduce the meter current
    D. steady the meter needle

19. A transit employee is required to make a written report of any unusual occurrences promptly.
    The BEST reason for requiring such promptness is that

    A. the report will tend to be more accurate as to facts
    B. the employee will not be as likely to forget to make the report
    C. there is always a tendency to do a better job under pressure
    D. the report may be too long if made at an employee's convenience

20. One thousand volts d.c. is to be tried out on the third-rail of an experimental section of a rapid-transit railroad to be built for another city. This voltage is higher than the third-rail voltage of the New York City subways by about _____ volts.

    A. 100   B. 200   C. 300   D. 400

21. The terminal voltage with batteries connected as shown is _____ volts.

    A. 0
    B. 1 1/2
    C. 3
    D. 6

    (4 CELLS EACH OF 1 1/2 VOLTS)

22. The voltage across terminal 1 and terminal 2 of the transformer connected as shown is _____ volts.

    A. 50
    B. 100
    C. 200
    D. 400

23. The total resistance in the circuit shown between terminal 1 and terminal 2 is _____ ohms.

    A. 1 1/2
    B. 6
    C. 9
    D. 15

24. The power used by the heater shown is _____ watts.
    A. 120
    B. 720
    C. 2400
    D. 4320

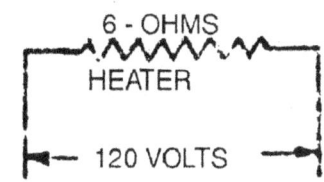

25. The current flowing through the 6-ohm resistor in the circuit shown is _____ amperes.
    A. 1
    B. 3
    C. 6
    D. 11

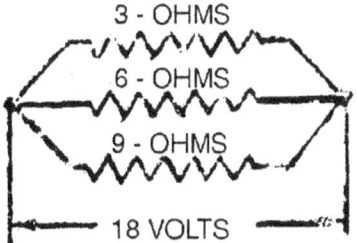

26. The voltage across the 30-ohm resistor in the circuit shown is _____ volts.
    A. 4
    B. 20
    C. 60
    D. 120

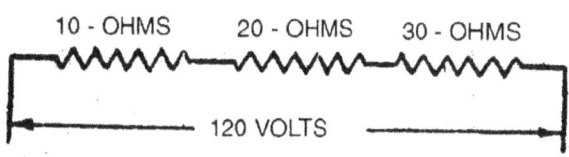

27. The current in the wire at the point indicated by the arrow is _____ amperes.

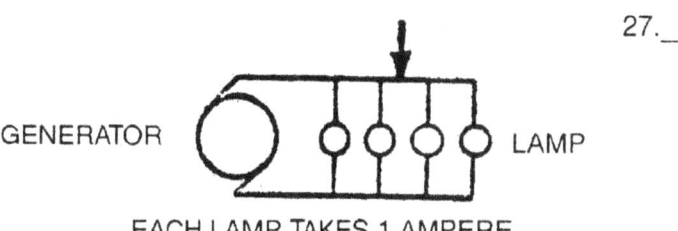

28. The sketch shows a head-on view of a three-pronged plug used with portable electrical power tools. Considering the danger of shock when using such tools, it is evident that the function of the U-shaped prong is to
    A. insure that the other two prongs enter the outlet with the proper polarity
    B. provide a half-voltage connection when doing light work
    C. prevent accidental pulling of the plug from the outlet
    D. connect the metallic shell of the tool motor to ground

29. The reading of the ammeter should be
    A. 4.0
    B. 2.0
    C. 1.0
    D. .05

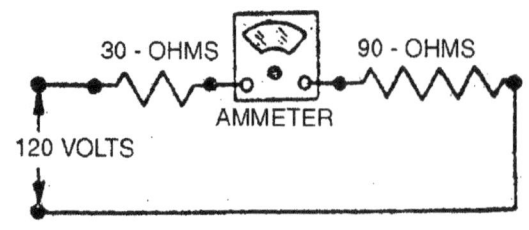

30. Applying your knowledge of electrical measuring instruments, it is *most likely* that the scale shown is for
    A. an ohmmeter
    B. a voltmeter
    C. an ammeter
    D. a wattmeter

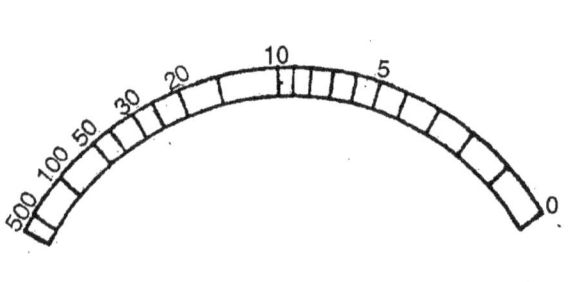

31. Assume that you have decided to test a sealed box having two terminals by using the hook-up shown. When you hold the test prods on the terminals, the voltmeter needle swings upscale and then quickly returns to zero. As an initial conclusion you would be CORRECT in assuming that the box contained a
    A. condenser
    B. choke
    C. rectifier
    D. resistor

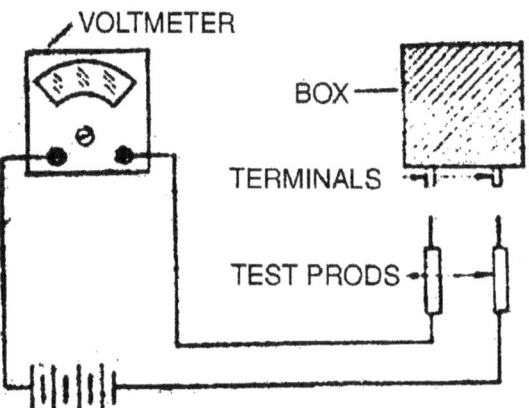

32. If each of the four 90° conduit elbows has the dimensions shown, the distance S is
    A. 20"
    B. 22"
    C. 24"
    D. 26"

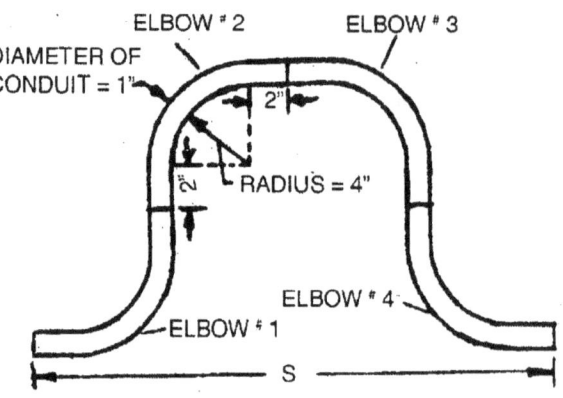

33. The purpose of the auxiliary blade on the knife switch shown is to
    A. delay the opening of the circuit when the handle is pulled open
    B. cut down arcing by opening the circuit quickly
    C. retain the blades in place
    D. increase the capacity of the switch

33.____

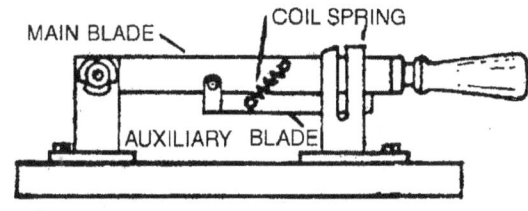

34. The sketch shows the four resistance dials and the multiplying dial of a resistance bridge. The four resistance dials can be set to any value of resistance up to 10,000 ohms, and the multiplier can be set at any of the nine points shown. In their present positions, the five pointers indicate a reading of
    A. 13.60
    B. 136.000
    C. 131.600
    D. 13.16

34.____

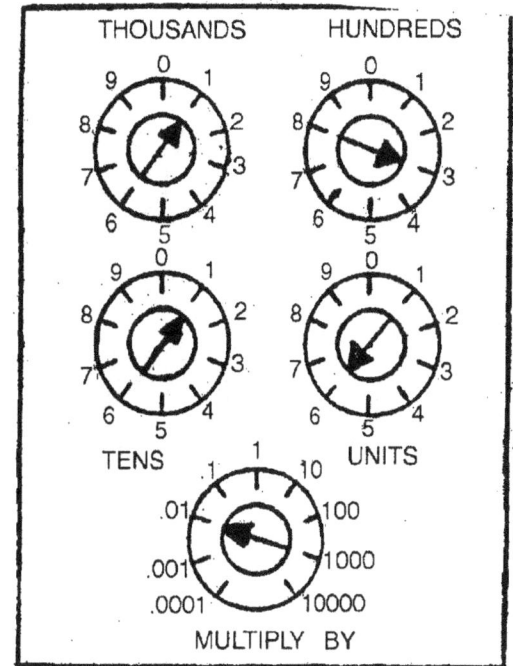

35. Regardless of the battery voltage, it is clear that the SMALLEST current is in the resistor having a resistance of
    A. 200 ohms
    B. 300 ohms
    C. 400 ohms
    D. 500 ohms

35.____

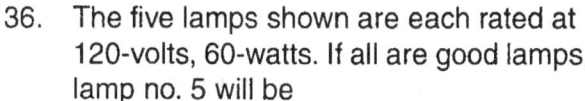

36. The five lamps shown are each rated at 120-volts, 60-watts. If all are good lamps, lamp no. 5 will be
    A. much brighter than normal
    B. about its normal brightness
    C. much dimmer than normal
    D. completely dark

36.____

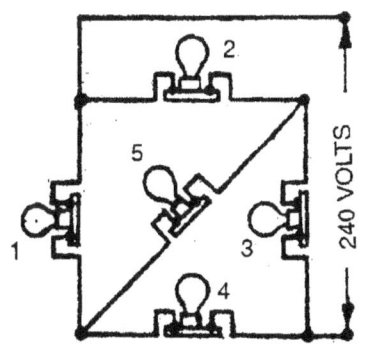

QUESTIONS 37-40.

Questions 37-40 inclusive show common electrical maintenance installation jobs. Each question shows four methods (A), (B), (C), and (D) of doing the particular job. Only ONE of the four methods is entirely CORRECT in accordance with good practice. For each question, examine the four sketches and select the sketch showing the correct method. PRINT on your answer sheet, in the correspondingly numbered question space, the letter given below your selected sketch.

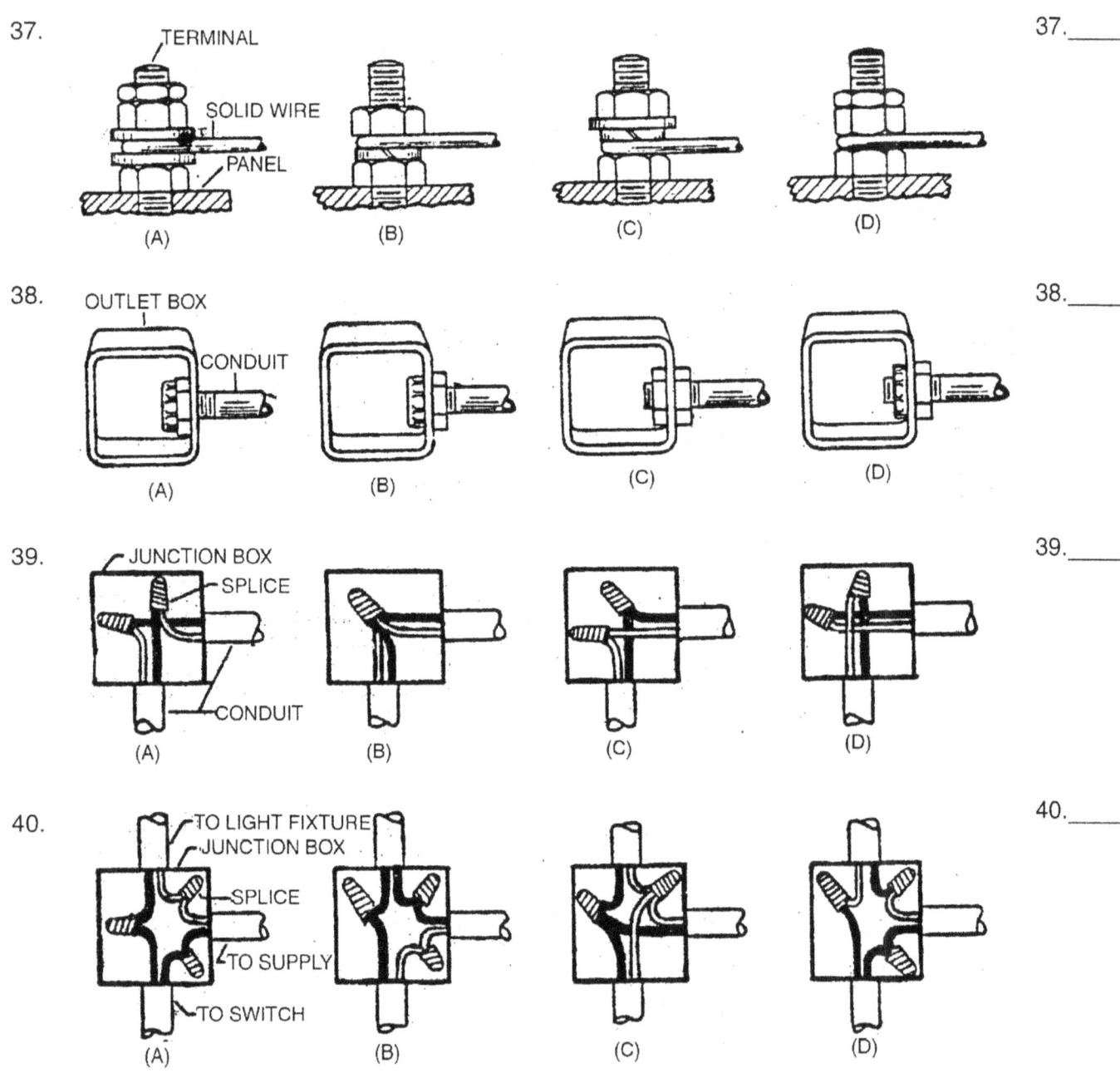

37. _____

38. _____

39. _____

40. _____

KEY (CORRECT ANSWERS)

1.	D	11.	B	21.	C	31.	A
2.	C	12.	C	22.	A	32.	D
3.	B	13.	B	23.	B	33.	B
4.	B	14.	A	24.	C	34.	D
5.	C	15.	A	25.	B	35.	C
6.	C	16.	C	26.	C	36.	D
7.	A	17.	D	27.	B	37.	A
8.	C	18.	C	28.	D	38.	B
9.	B	19.	A	29.	C	39.	C
10.	B	20.	D	30.	A	40.	A

ELECTRIC MOTOR AND GENERATOR REPAIR

CONTENTS

	Page
I. TROUBLESHOOTING DATA FOR GENERATORS AND MOTORS	1
<u>Section I. DC Generators</u>	1
1. Failure to Build up Voltage	1
2. Output Voltage too Low	1
3. Output Voltage too High	1
4. Armature Overheats	1
5. Field Coils Overheat	2
6. Sparking at Brushes	2
<u>Section II. DC Motors</u>	2
7. Failure to Start	2
8. Stops After Running a Short Time	2
9. Attempts to Start, but Overload Relays Trip Out	2
10. Runs too Slow	3
11. Runs too Fast Under Load	3
12. Sparking at Brushes	3
13. Overheating	3
<u>Section III. AC Generators</u>	3
14. Noisy Operation	3
15. Overheating	3
16. No Output Voltage	3
17. Output Voltage Unsteady	4
18. Output Voltage too High	4
19. Frequency Incorrect or Fluctuating	4
20. Voltage Hunting	4
21. Stator Overheats in Spots	4
22. Field Overheating	4
23. Alternator Produces Shock When Touched	4
<u>Section IV. AC Induction Motors</u>	4
24. Failure to Start	4
25. Noisy Operation	4
26. Overheating	5
<u>Section V. AC Wound Rotor Motors</u>	5
27. Runs Slow with External Resistance Cutout	5
<u>Section VI. AC Synchronous Motors</u>	5
28. Failure to Start	5
29. Runs Slow	5
30. Failure to Pull into Step	5
31. No Field Excitation	5
32. Pulls Out of Step, or Trips Breakers	6
33. Hunting	6
34. Stator Overheats in Spots	6
35. Field Overheats	6
36. Overheating	6
<u>Section VII. AC Repulsion Induction Motors</u>	6
37. Failure to Start	6
38. Runs Slow	7
39. Overheating	7
40. Noisy Operation	7
41. Motor Produces Shock when Touched	7

continued ....

ELECTRIC MOTOR AND GENERATOR REPAIR (cont'd)

CONTENTS

	Page
Section VIII. AC Split-Phase, Capacitor-Start, and Transformer-Capacitor Motors	7
42. Failure to Start	7
43. Overheating	7
44. Noisy Operation	8
II. TROUBLESHOOTING DATA FOR DC AND AC CONTROLLERS	9
Section I. DC Controllers	9
45. Failure to Close	9
46. Failure to Open	9
47. Sluggish Operation	9
48. Erratic Operation (Unwanted openings and closures, and failure of overload protection)	9
49. Overheating of Coils	10
50. Contacts Welded Together	10
51. Overheating of Contacts	10
52. Excessive Arcing of Contacts	10
53. Pitting or Corroding of Contacts	11
Section II. AC Controllers	11
54. Failure to Close	11
55. Failure to Open	11
56. Sluggish Operation	11
57. Erratic Operation (Unwanted openings and closures, and failure of overload protection)	12
58. Overheating of Coils	12
59. Contacts Welded Together	12
60. Overheating or Contacts	12
61. Arcing at Contacts	13
62. Pitting or Corroding of Contacts	13
63. Noisy Operation (Hum or Chatter)	13
64. Vibration After Repairs	13

ELECTRIC MOTOR AND GENERATOR REPAIR

I. TROUBLESHOOTING DATA FOR GENERATORS AND MOTORS

Section I. DC GENERATORS

1. Failure to Build up Voltage

Probable cause	*Remedy*
Voltmeter not operating	Check output voltage with separate voltmeter. Replace voltmeter.
Open field resistor	Repair or replace resistor.
Open field circuit	Check coils for open and loose connections. Replace the defective coil or coils. Tighten or solder loose connections.
Absence of residual magnetism in a self-excited generator.	Flash the field.
Dirty commutator	Clean or dress commutator.
High mica	Undercut mica.
Brushes not making proper contact	Free, if binding in holders. Replace and reseat if worn.
Newly seated brushes not contacting sufficient area on the commutator.	Run in by reducing load and use a brush-seating stone.
Armature shorted internally, or to ground	Remove, test, and repair or replace.
Grounded or shorted field coil	Test, and repair or replace.
Shorted filtering capacitor	Replace.
Open filter choke	Replace.
Open ammeter shunt	Replace ammeter and shunt.
Broken brush shunts or pigtails	Replace brushes.

2. Output Voltage too Low

Probable cause	*Remedy*
Prime mover speed too low	Check speed with tachometer. Adjust governor on prime mover.
Brushes not seated properly	Run in with partial load, use brush-seating stone.
Commutator is dirty or film is too heavy	Clean, or if film is too heavy, replace brushes with a complete set of proper grade.
Field resistor not properly adjusted	Adjust field strength. Tighten all connections. Make shim adjustment.
Reversed field coil or armature connection	Check and connect properly.

3. Output Voltage Too High

Probable cause	*Remedy*
Prime mover speed too high	Check speed with tachometer. Adjust governor on prime mover.
Faulty voltage regulator	Adjust or replace.

4. Armature Overheats

Probable cause	*Remedy*
Overloaded	Check meter readings against nameplate ratings. Reduce load.
Excessive brush pressure	Adjust pressure or replace tension springs.
Couplings not alined	Aline units properly

Probable cause	Remedy
End bells improperly positioned	Assemble correctly
Bent shaft	Straighten or replace
Armature coil shorted	Repair or replace armature
Armature rubbing or striking poles	Check for bent shaft, loose or worn bearings. Straighten and realine shaft. Replace bearings, tighten pole pieces, or replace armature.
Clogged air passages (poor ventilation)	Clean equipment
Repeated changes in load of great magnitude. (Improper design for the application).	Generator should be used with a steady load application.
Unequal brush tension	Equalize brush tension
Broken shunts or pigtails	Replace brushes
Open in field rheostat	Repair or replace rheostat

5. Field Coils Overheat

Probable cause	Remedy
Shorted or grounded coils	Repair or replace
Clogged air passages (poor ventilation)	Clean equipment. Remove obstructions.
Overload (compound generator)	Check meter reading against nameplate rating. Reduce load.

6. Sparking at Brushes

Probable cause	Remedy
Overload	Check meter readings against nameplate ratings. Reduce load.
Brushes off neutral plane	Adjust brush rigging.
Dirty brushes and commutator	Clean brushes and commutator.
High mica	Undercut mica.
Rough or eccentric commutator	Resurface commutator.
Open circuit in the armature	Repair or replace armature.
Grounded, open- or short-circuited field winding	Repair or replace defective coil or coils.
Insufficient brush pressure	Adjust or replace tension springs.
Brushes sticking in the holders	Clean holders. Sand brushes.

Section II. DC MOTORS

7. Failure to Start

Probable cause	Remedy
Open circuit in the control	Check for open. Replace open resistor or fuse.
Low supply voltage	Check with voltmeter and apply proper voltage.
Frozen bearing	Replace bearing and recondition shaft.
Overload	Reduce load or use larger motor.
Excessive friction	Check for air gap, bent shaft, loose or worn bearings, misalined end bells. Straighten shaft, replace bearings, tighten pole pieces, aline end bells.

8. Stops After Running a Short Time

Probable cause	Remedy
Failure of supply voltage	Apply proper voltage, replace fuses, or reset overload relay.
Overload	Check meter readings against nameplate ratings. Reduce load.
Ambient temperature too high	Ventilate space to reduce ambient temperature.
Overload relays set too low for application	Adjust relays for the application.

9. Attempts to Start, But Overload Relays Trip Out

Probable cause	Remedy
Motor field weak or non-existent	Check field circuit. Repair or replace defective field coils. Tighten all connections.
Overload	Check meter readings against nameplate ratings. Replace motor with one suitable to the application.
Relays adjusted too low for the application	Adjust relays for the application.

10. Runs too Slow

Probable cause	Remedy
Line voltage low	Apply proper voltage.
Bushes ahead of neutral plane	Adjust brush rigging.
Overload	Check meter reading against nameplate readings. Reduce load.

11. Runs too Fast under Load

Probable cause	Remedy
Weak field	Check field circuit. Replace open coils or open starter resistors.
Line voltage too high	Reduce line voltage.
Brushes off adjustment with neutral plane	Adjust brush rigging.

12. Sparking at Brushes

Probable cause	Remedy
Same as dc generator (par. 6)	Same as dc generator (par. 6).

13. Overheating

Probable cause	Remedy
Same as dc generator (par. 4 and 5)	Same as dc generator (par. 4 and 5).

Section III. AC GENERATORS

14. Noisy Operation

Probable cause	Remedy
Unbalanced load	Balance load.
Coupling loose or misalined	Reline coupling and tighten.
Improper air gap	Check for bent shaft, loose or worn bearings. Straighten and realine shaft. Replace bearings.
Loose laminations	Tighten bolts. Dip in varnish and bake.

15. Overheating

Probable cause	Remedy
Overloaded	Check meter readings against nameplate ratings. Reduce load.
Unbalanced load	Balance load.
Open load-line fuse	Replace fuse.
Restricted ventilation	Clean, and remove obstructions to ventilation.
Rotor winding short-circuited, open-circuited, or grounded.	Check, and replace defective coil or coils.
Stator winding short-circuited, open-circuited, or grounded.	Check, and replace defective coil or coils.
Bearings	Check for worn, loose, dry, or overlubricated bearings. Replace worn or loose bearings, lubricate dry bearings, relieve overlubrication.

16. No Output Voltage

Probable cause	Remedy
Stator coils open- or short-circuited	Check, and replace defective coil or coils.
Rotor coils open- or short-circuited	Check, and replace defective coil or coils.
Shorted sliprings	Disconnect field coils and check ring-insulation resistance with megger. Repair.
Internal moisture	Check with megger and dry windings.
No dc voltage at the slipring brushes. (No dc exciter voltage.)	Check for defective switch or blown fuse in exciter feeder lines. Repair switch or replace fuses. Check feeder cables for opens or shorts. Repair connections or replace cables. Refer to FAILURE TO BUILD UP VOLTAGE (par. 1).
Voltmeter defective	Check with a voltmeter known to be working properly. Replace.
Ammeter shunt open	Replace ammeter and shunt.

17. Output Voltage Unsteady

Probable cause — *Remedy*

Poor commutation at sliprings .... Clean sliprings and brushes. Reseat brushes.
Loose terminal connections .... Clean and tighten all connections and contacts.
Maladjusted voltage regulator and speed governor ...... Readjust speed governor and voltage regulator.

18. Output Voltage too High

Probable cause — *Remedy*

Overspeeding .... Adjust speed-governing device.
Overexcited .... Adjust voltage regulator.
Delta-connected stator open on one leg .... Remake connection, repair or replace defective coil or coils.

19. Frequency Incorrect or Fluctuating

Probable cause — *Remedy*

Speed incorrect or fluctuating .... Adjust speed-governing device.
Dc excitation fluctuating .... Adjust belt tension of exciter generator.

20. Voltage Hunting

Probable cause — *Remedy*

External field resistance in total out position .... Readjust resistance.
Voltage regulator contacts dirty .... Clean and reset contact points.

21. Stator Overheats in Spots

Probable cause — *Remedy*

Short-circuited phase winding .... Check and replace defective coils.
Rotor off center. (Improper air gap.) .... Check for bent shaft, loose or worn bearings. Straighten and realine shaft. Replace bearings.
Unbalanced winding circuits .... Balance winding circuits.
Loose winding connections .... Tighten winding connections.
Wrong phase polarity connections .... Correct connections for proper phase polarity.

22. Field Overheating

Probable cause — *Remedy*

Shorted field coil or coils .... Check and replace defective coil or coils.
Dc excitation current too high .... Reduce exciter current by adjusting dc voltage regulator.
Clogged air passages (poor ventilation) .... Clean equipment. Remove obstructions.

23. Alternator Produces Shock when Touched

Probable cause — *Remedy*

Reversed stator field coil .... Check polarity. Make correction to connections.
Static charges or grounded stator field coil .... Check generator frame-ground connection or connections, clean and tighten. Repair or replace stator field coil.

Section IV. AC INDUCTION MOTORS

24. Failure to Start

Probable cause — *Remedy*

Circuit breaker or fuse open .... Check for grounds. Close breaker or replace fuse.
Overload relay open .... Wait until motor cools and relay closes.
Low supply voltage .... Apply correct voltage.
Stator or rotor windings open or shorted .... Check and replace shorted coil or coils.
Winding grounded .... Check and replace grounded coil or coils.
Overload .... Check meter readings against nameplate ratings. Reduce or install larger motor.

25. Noisy Operation

Probable cause — *Remedy*

Unbalanced load or coupling misalinement .... Balance load and check alinement.
Air gap not uniform .... Center rotor by replacing bearing.
Lamination loose .... Tighten bolts. Dip in varnish and bake (chapter 4, par. 70). Repeat several times.
Coupling loose .... Tighten.

26. Overheating

Probable cause	Remedy
Overloaded	Check meter readings against nameplate ratings. Reduce load.
Electrical unbalance	Balance supply voltage.
Open fuse	Replace line fuse.
Restricted ventilation	Clean. Remove obstructions.
Rotor winding shorted, open, or grounded	Check and replace defective coil or coils.
Stator winding shorted, open, or grounded	Check and replace defective coil or coils.
Bearings	Check for worn, loose, dry, or overlubricated bearings. Replace worn or loose bearings, lubricate dry bearings, relieve overlubrication.

Section V. AC WOUND ROTOR MOTORS

27. Runs Slow with External Resistance Cutout

Probable cause	Remedy
Cables to control box have insufficient current-carrying capacity.	Replace with larger cables.
Open circuits in rotor, cables, or controls	Clean, remake connections, and repair.
Excessive brush sparking	Clean sliprings and reseat brushes.

Section VI. AC SYNCHRONOUS MOTORS

28. Failure to Start

Probable cause	Remedy
Open fuse	Replace fuse.
Faulty starter	Check and repair or replace faulty contacts or contactor coils.
Low supply voltage	Apply correct voltage.
Bearings	Check for bent shaft or worn, loose, dry, or overlubricated bearings. Replace and realine bent shaft. Replace worn and loose bearings, lubricate dry bearings, relieve overlubrication.
Overloaded	Check meter readings against nameplate ratings. Reduce load or install larger motor.
Stator coil open or shorted	Repair or replace coil or coils.
Field exciter current is being applied	Make sure that field contactors are open, and that field-discharge resistors are connected.

29. Runs Slow

Probable cause	Remedy
Overloaded	Check meter readings against nameplate. Reduce load or install larger motor.
Low supply voltage	Apply correct voltage.
Field excited too soon	Adjust time-delay relay so that exciter current will not be applied until rotor reaches synchronous speed.

30. Failure to Pull into Step

Probable cause	Remedy
No field excitation. Open rotor coils. Exciter inoperative. Faulty field contactor.	Tighten or solder open or loose connections. Repair or replace defective rotor coils. Be sure field contactor is operating properly.
Overloaded	Check meter readings against nameplate ratings. Reduce load or install larger motor.

31. No Field Excitation

Probable cause	Remedy
Grounded or open rotor coil	Repair or replace rotor coil or coils.
Grounded or short sliprings	Check and reinsulate.
No output from exciter	See dc generator (par. 1).

32. Pulls out of Step, or Trips Breakers

Probable cause	Remedy
Low exciter voltage	Readjust voltage regulator on exciter to increase voltage.
Intermittently open or shorted cables	Check, and replace defective cables.
Reversed field coil	Check polarity. Change coil leads.
Low supply voltage	Increase voltage if possible. Raise excitation voltage.

33. Hunting

Probable cause	Remedy
Fluctuating load	Increase or decrease size of flywheel on load or loads. Increase or decrease excitation current.
Uneven commutator	Recondition commutator.

34. Stator Overheats in Spots

Probable cause	Remedy
Open phase coil	Check and repair or replace faulty coil or coils.
Rotor not centered	Check for bent shaft, loose or worn bearings. Straighten and realine shaft. Replace bearings.
Unbalanced circuits	Repair loose connections, or correct wrong internal connections.
Shorted coil	Check and replace faulty coil or coils.

35. Field Overheats

Probable cause	Remedy
Shorted field coil	Check and replace faulty coil or coils.
Excitation current too high	Reduce exciter current by adjusting dc voltage regulator.

36. Overheating

Probable cause	Remedy
Overloaded	Check meter readings against nameplate ratings. Reduce load or install larger motor.
Underexcited rotor	Adjust to rated excitation.
Improper ventilation	Remove obstructions and clean air ducts.
Improper supply voltage	Adjust to rated voltage.
Reverse field coil	Check polarity. Change coil leads.

Section VII. AC REPULSION-INDUCTION MOTORS

37. Failure to Start

Probable cause	Remedy
Open fuse	Replace fuse.
Overloaded	Check meter readings against nameplate ratings. Reduce load or install larger motor.
Low supply voltage. Lead wires insufficient current capacity.	Apply correct voltage. Install larger lead wires.
Stator coil open	Check and replace open coil or coils.
Stator coil shorted	Check and replace shorted coil or coils.
Stator coil grounded	Check and replace defective coil or coils.
Centrifugal mechanism not operating properly	Disassemble, clean, inspect, adjust, repair or replace.
Incorrect brush setting	Locate neutral plane by shifting brushes until there is no rotation when current is applied. Shift brushes in the direction of the desired rotation, 1½ bars from neutral on 4-pole motors of ½ hp and smaller, and 1¾ bars on larger 4-pole motors. On 2-pole motors, set ⅓ bar farther than setting given above.
Bearings	Check for bent shaft or worn, loose, dry, or overlubricated bearing. Straighten and realine bent shaft. Replace worn and loose bearings, lubricate dry bearings, relieve overlubrication.

38. Runs Slow

Probable cause	Remedy
Overloaded	Check meter readings against nameplate rating.
Centrifugal mechanism not operating properly	Disassemble and clean.
Bearings binding	Clean and lubricate bearings.

39. Overheating

Probable cause	Remedy
Overloaded	Check meter readings against nameplate ratings. Reduce load or install larger motor.
Incorrect supply voltage	Apply correct voltage.
Centrifugal mechanism not operating properly	Disassemble, clean, inspect. Repair, adjust, or replace.
Bearings	Check for bent shaft, or worn, loose, dry, or overlubricated bearings. Straighten and realine bent shaft. Replace worn or loose bearings, lubricate dry bearings, relieve overlubrication.

40. Noisy Operation

Probable cause	Remedy
Bearings	Check for bent shaft, or worn, loose, dry, or overlubricated bearings. Straighten and realine bent shaft. Replace worn or loose bearings, lubricate dry bearings, relieve overlubrication.
Excessive end play	Adjust end-play takeup screw, or add thrust washers to shaft.
Motor not alined properly with driven machine	Realine.
Loose motor mounting and accessories	Tighten all loose components.

41. Motor Produces Shock when Touched

Probable cause	Remedy
Grounded stator coil	Replace defective coil or coils. Check motor-frame connection or connections to ground. Clean and tighten.
Static charge	Check motor-frame connection or connections to ground. Clean and tighten.

Section VIII. AC SPLIT-PHASE, CAPACITOR-START, AND TRANSFORMER-CAPACITOR MOTORS

42. Failure to Start

Probable cause	Remedy
Open fuse	Replace fuse.
Low supply voltage	Apply correct voltage.
Stator coil open	Replace open coil or coils.
Centrifugal mechanism not operating properly	Disassemble, clean, inspect. Adjust, repair, or replace.
Defective capacitor	Replace capacitor.
Stator coil grounded	Check and replace grounded coil or coils.
Bearings	Check for bent shaft, or worn, loose, dry, or overlubricated bearings. Straighten and realine bent shaft. Replace worn or loose bearings, relieve overlubrication.
Overloaded	Check meter readings against nameplate ratings. Reduce load or install larger motor.

43. Overheating

Probable cause	Remedy
Shorted coil	Replace shorted coil or coils.
Centrifugal mechanism not operating properly	Disassemble, clean, inspect. Adjust, repair, or replace.
Incorrect voltage	Apply correct voltage.
Overloaded	Check meter readings against nameplate ratings. Reduce load or install larger motor.
Bearings	Check for bent shaft, or worn, loose, dry, or overlubricated bearings. Straighten and realine bent shaft, replace worn or loose bearings, lubricate dry bearings, relieve overlubrication.

44. Noisy Operation

Probable cause	Remedy
Worn bearings	Replace. Realine.
Shaft bent	Straighten shaft. Realine or replace rotor.
Excessive end play	Adjust screw of end-play takeup device, or put shim washers on shaft between end bells and rotor.
Loose motor mounts or accessories	Tighten all loose components.

11. TROUBLESHOOTING DATA FOR DC AND AC CONTROLLERS

Section I. DC CONTROLLERS

45. Failure to Close

Probable cause	*Remedy*
No power	Check power source. Replace faulty fuses.
Low voltage	Check power-supply voltage. Apply correct voltage.
Inadequate lead wires	Install lead wires of proper size.
Loose connections	Tighten all connections.
Open connections and broken wiring	Locate and repair or replace. Remove dirt from controller contacts.
Contacts affected by long idleness or high operating temperature.	Clean and adjust.
Contacts affected by chemical fumes or salty atmosphere.	Replace with oil-immersed contacts.
Inadequate contact pressure	Replace contacts and adjust spring tension.
Open circuit breaker	Check circuit wiring for possible fault.
Defective coil	Replace with new coil.
Overload-relay contact latched open	Operate hand- or electric-reset.

46. Failure to Open

Probable cause	*Remedy*
Interlock does not open circuit	Check control-circuit wiring for possible fault. Test and repair.
Holding circuit grounded	Test and repair or replace grounded parts.
Misalinement of parts; contacts apparently held together by residual magnetism.	Realine and test for free movement by hand. Magnetic sticking rarely occurs unless caused by excessive mechanical friction or misalinement of moving parts.
Contacts welded together	See paragraph 50, below.

47. Sluggish Operation

Probable cause	*Remedy*
Spring tension too strong	Adjust for proper spring tension.
Low voltage	Check power-supply voltage. Apply correct voltage.
Operating in wrong position	Remount in correct operating position.
Excessive friction	Realine and test for free movement by hand. Clean pivots.
Rusty parts due to long periods of idleness	Clean and renew rusty parts.
Sticky moving parts	Wipe off all accumulations of oil and dirt. Bearings do not need lubrication.
Misalinement of parts	Check for proper alinement. Realine to reduce friction, and test for free movement by hand.

48. Erratic Operation (Unwanted openings and closures, and failure of overload protection)

Probable cause	*Remedy*
Short circuits	Test and repair or replace defective parts.
Grounds	Test and repair or replace defective parts.

Probable cause	Remedy
Sneak currents	These are usually caused by intermittent grounds or short circuits in the machines or wiring circuit. Test and replace faulty parts or wiring.
Loose connections	Tighten all connections. Eliminate any vibrations or rapid temperature changes that may occur in close proximity to the controller.

49. Overheating of Coils

Probable cause	Remedy
Shorted coil	Replace coil.
High ambient temperature or poor ventilation	Relocate controller, use forced ventilation, or replace with suitable type controller.
High voltage	Check for shorted control resistor. Check power-supply voltage. Apply correct voltage.
High current	Check current rating of controller. Check for high voltage, above. If necessary, replace with suitable type controller.
Loose connections	Tighten all connections. Check for undue vibrations in vicinity.
Excessive collection of dirt and grime	Clean but do not reoil parts. If covers do not fit tightly, realine and adjust fasteners.
High humidity, extremely dirty atmosphere, excessive condensation, and rapid temperature changes.	Use oil-immersed controller or dusttight enclosures.

50. Contacts Welded Together

Probable cause	Remedy
Improper application	Check load conditions and replace with a suitable type controller.
Excessive temperature	Smooth off contact surface to remove concentrated hot spots.
Excessive binding of contact tip upon closing	Adjust spring pressure.
Contacts close without enough spring pressure	Replace worn contacts. Adjust or replace weak springs. Check armature overtravel.
Sluggish operation	See paragraph 47, above.
Rapid, momentary, touching of contacts without enough pressure.	Smooth contacts. Adjust weak springs. Where controller has "JOG" or "INCH" control button, operate this less rapidly.

51. Overheating of Contacts

Probable cause	Remedy
Inadequate spring pressure	Replace worn contacts. Adjust or replace weak springs.
Contacts overloaded	Check load data with controller rating. Replace with correct size contactor.
Dirty contacts	Clean and smooth contacts.
High humidity, extremely dirty atmosphere, excessive condensation, and rapid temperature changes.	See paragraph 49, above.
High ambient temperature or poor ventilation	See paragraph 49, above.
Chronic arcing	Adjust or replace arc chutes. If arcing persists, replace with a more suitable controller.
Rough contact surface	Clean and smooth contacts. Check alinement.
Continuous vibration when contacts are closed	Change or improve mounting of controller.
Oxidation of contacts	Keep clean, reduce excessive temperature, or use oil-immersed contacts.

52. Excessive Arcing of Contacts

Probable cause	Remedy
Arc not confined to proper path	Adjust or renew arc chutes. If arcing persists, replace with more suitable controller.
Inadequate spring pressure	Replace worn contacts. Adjust or replace weak springs.
Slow in opening	Remove excessive friction. Adjust spring tension. Renew weak springs. See paragraph 47, above.
Faulty blowout coil or connection	Check and replace coil. Tighten connection.
Excessive inductance in load circuit	Adjust load or replace with proper size controller.
Faulty capacitor	Replace with new capacitor.

53. Pitting or Corroding of Contacts

Probable cause	Remedy
Too little surface contact	Clean contacts and adjust springs.
Service too severe	Check load conditions and replace with correct size controller.
Corrosive atmosphere	Use airtight enclosure. In extreme cases, use oil-immersed contacts.
Continuous vibration when contacts are closed	Change, or improve, mounting of controller.
Oxidation of contacts	Keep clean, reduce excessive temperature, or use oil-immersed contacts.

Section II. AC CONTROLLERS

54. Failure to Close

Probable cause	Remedy
No power	Check power source. Replace faulty fuses.
Low voltage	Check power-supply voltage. Apply correct voltage. Check for low power factor.
Inadequate lead wires	Install lead wires of proper size.
Loose connections	Tighten all connections.
Open connections and broken wiring	Locate opens and repair or replace wiring. Remove dirt from controller contacts.
Contacts affected by long idleness or high operating temperature.	Clean and adjust.
Contacts affected by chemical fumes or salty atmosphere.	Replace with oil-immersed contacts.
Inadequate contact pressure	Replace contacts and adjust spring tension.
Open circuit breaker	Check circuit wiring for possible fault.
Defective coil	Replace with new coil.
Overload-relay contact latched open	Operate hand- or electric-reset.

55. Failure to Open

Probable cause	Remedy
Interlock does not open circuit	Check control-circuit wiring for possible fault. Test and repair.
Holding circuit grounded	Test and repair or replace grounded parts.
Misalinement of parts; contacts apparently held together by residual magnetism.	Realine and test for free movement by hand. Magnetic sticking rarely occurs unless caused by excessive mechanical friction or misalinement of moving parts. Wipe off pole faces to remove accumulation of oil.
Contacts welded together	See paragraph 59, below.

56. Sluggish Operation

Probable cause	Remedy
Spring tension too strong	Adjust for proper spring tension.
Low voltage	Check power-supply voltage. Apply correct voltage.
Operating in wrong position	Remount in correct operating position.
Excessive friction	Realine and test for free movement by hand. Clean pivots.
Rusty parts due to long periods of idleness	Clean or renew rusty parts.
Sticky moving parts	Wipe off all accumulations of oil and dirt. Bearings do not need lubrication.
Misalinement of parts	Check for proper alinement. Realine to reduce friction and test for free movement by hand.

57. Erratic Operation (Unwanted openings and closures and failure of overload protection)

Probable cause — *Remedy*

Short circuits .... Test and repair or replace defective parts.

Grounds .... Test and repair or replace defective parts.

Sneak currents .... These are usually caused by intermittent grounds or short circuits in the machines or wiring circuit. Test and replace faulty parts or wiring.

Loose connections .... Tighten all connections. Eliminate any vibrations or rapid temperature changes that may occur in close proximity to the controller.

58. Overheating of Coils

Probable cause — *Remedy*

Shorted coil .... Replace coil.

High ambient temperature or poor ventilation .... Relocate controller, use forced ventilation, or replace with suitable type controller.

High voltage .... Check for shorted control resistor. Check power-supply voltage. Apply correct voltage.

High current .... Check current rating of controller. Make check for high voltage, above. If necessary, replace with suitable type controller.

Loose connections .... Tighten all connections. Check for undue vibrations in vicinity.

Excessive collection of dirt and grime .... Clean but do not reoil parts. If covers do not fit tightly, realine and adjust fasteners.

High humidity, extremely dirty atmosphere, excessive condensation, and rapid temperature changes. .... Use oil-immersed controller or dusttight enclosures.

Operating on wrong frequency .... Replace with coil of proper frequency rating.

DC instead of ac coil .... Replace with ac coil.

Too frequent operation .... Adjust to apply larger control.

Open armature gap .... Adjust spring tension. Eliminate excessive friction or remove any blocking in gap.

59. Contacts Welded Together

Probable cause — *Remedy*

Improper application .... Check load conditions and replace with a more suitable type controller.

Excessive temperature .... Smooth off contact surface to remove concentrated hot spots.

Excessive binding of contact tip upon closing .... Adjust spring pressure.

Contacts close without enough spring pressure ...... Replace worn contacts. Adjust or replace weak springs. Check armature overtravel.

Sluggish operation .... See paragraph 56, above.

Rapid, momentary, touching of contacts without enough pressure. .... Smooth contacts. Adjust weak springs. Where controller has "JOG" or "INCH" control button, operate this less rapidly.

60. Overheating or Contacts

Probable cause — *Remedy*

Inadequate spring pressure .... Replace worn contacts. Adjust or replace weak springs.

Contacts overloaded .... Check load data with controller rating. Replace with correct size contactor.

Dirty contacts .... Clean and smooth contacts.

High humidity, extremely dirty atmosphere, excessive condensation, and rapid temperature changes. .... See paragraph 58, above.

High ambient temperature or poor ventilation .... See paragraph 58, above.

Chronic arcing .... Adjust or replace arc chutes. If arcing persists, replace with a more suitable controller.

Probable cause — *Remedy*

Rough contact surfaces .... Clean and smooth contacts. Check alinement.
Continuous vibration when contacts are closed .... Change or improve mounting of controller.
Oxidation of contacts .... Keep clean, reduce excessive temperature, or use oil-immersed contacts.

61. Arcing at Contacts

Probable cause — *Remedy*

Arc not confined to proper path .... Adjust or renew arc chutes. If arcing persists, replace with more suitable controller.
Inadequate spring pressure .... Replace worn contacts. Adjust or replace weak springs.
Slow in opening .... Remove excessive friction. Adjust spring tension. Renew weak springs. See paragraph 56, above.
Faulty blowout coil or connection .... Check and replace coil. Tighten connection.
Excessive inductance in load circuit .... Adjust load or replace with more suitable controller.

62. Pitting or Corroding of Contacts

Probable cause — *Remedy*

Too little surface contact .... Clean contacts and adjust springs.
Service too severe .... Check load conditions and replace with more suitable controller.
Corrosive atmosphere .... Use airtight enclosure. In extreme cases, use oil-immersed contacts.
Continuous vibration when contacts are closed .... Change or improve mounting of controller.
Oxidation of contacts .... Keep clean, reduce excessive temperature, or use oil-immersed contacts.

63. Noisy Operation (Hum or Chatter)

Probable cause — *Remedy*

Poor fit at pole face .... Realine and adjust pole faces.
Broken or defective shading coil .... Replace coil.
Loose coil .... Check coil. If correct size, shim coil until tight.
Worn parts .... Replace with new parts.

64. Vibration After Repairs

Probable cause — *Remedy*

Misalinement of parts .... Realine parts and test for free movement by hand.
Loose mounting .... Tighten mounting bolts.
Incorrect coil .... Replace with proper coil.
Too much play in moving parts .... Shim parts for proper tightness and clearance.

ELECTRICAL TERMS AND FORMULAS

CONTENTS

	Page
TERMS	1
Agonic ...... Dielectric	1
Diode ...... Lead	2
Line of Force ...... Resistor	3
Retentivity ...... Wattmeter	4
FORMULAS	4
Ohm's Law for D-C Circuits	4
Resistors in Series	4
Resistors in Parallel	4
R-L Circuit Time Constant	5
R-C Circuit Time Constant	5
Comparison of Units in Electric and Magnetic Circuits	5
Capacitors in Series	5
Capacitors in Parallel	5
Capacitive Reactance	5
Impedance in an R-C Circuit (Series)	5
Inductors in Series	5
Inductors in Parallel	5
Inductive Reactance	5
Q of a Coil	5
Impedance of an R-L Circuit (Series)	5
Impedance with R, C, and L in Series	5
Parallel Circuit Impedance	5
Sine-Wave Voltage Relationships	5
Power in A-C Circuit	6
Transformers	6
Three-Phase Voltage and Current Relationships	6
GREEK ALPHABET	7
Alpha ...... Omega	7
COMMON ABBREVIATIONS AND LETTER SYMBOLS	8
Alternating Current (noun) ...... Watt	8

ELECTRICAL TERMS AND FORMULAS

Terms

AGONIC.—An imaginary line of the earth's surface passing through points where the magnetic declination is 0°; that is, points where the compass points to true north.

AMMETER.—An instrument for measuring the amount of electron flow in amperes.

AMPERE.—The basic unit of electrical current.

AMPERE-TURN.—The magnetizing force produced by a current of one ampere flowing through a coil of one turn.

AMPLIDYNE.—A rotary magnetic or dynamoelectric amplifier used in servomechanism and control applications.

AMPLIFICATION.—The process of increasing the strength (current, power, or voltage) of a signal.

AMPLIFIER.—A device used to increase the signal voltage, current, or power, generally composed of a vacuum tube and associated circuit called a stage. It may contain several stages in order to obtain a desired gain.

AMPLITUDE.—The maximum instantaneous value of an alternating voltage or current, measured in either the positive or negative direction.

ARC.—A flash caused by an electric current ionizing a gas or vapor.

ARMATURE.—The rotating part of an electric motor or generator. The moving part of a relay or vibrator.

ATTENUATOR.—A network of resistors used to reduce voltage, current, or power delivered to a load.

AUTOTRANSFORMER.—A transformer in which the primary and secondary are connected together in one winding.

BATTERY.—Two or more primary or secondary cells connected together electrically. The term does not apply to a single cell.

BREAKER POINTS.—Metal contacts that open and close a circuit at timed intervals.

BRIDGE CIRCUIT.—The electrical bridge circuit is a term referring to any one of a variety of electric circuit networks, one branch of which, the "bridge" proper, connects two points of equal potential and hence carries no current when the circuit is properly adjusted or balanced.

BRUSH.—The conducting material, usually a block of carbon, bearing against the commutator or sliprings through which the current flows in or out.

BUS BAR.—A primary power distribution point connected to the main power source.

CAPACITOR.—Two electrodes or sets of electrodes in the form of plates, separated from each other by an insulating material called the dielectric.

CHOKE COIL.—A coil of low ohmic resistance and high impedance to alternating current.

CIRCUIT.—The complete path of an electric current.

CIRCUIT BREAKER.—An electromagnetic or thermal device that opens a circuit when the current in the circuit exceeds a predetermined amount. Circuit breakers can be reset.

CIRCULAR MIL.—An area equal to that of a circle with a diameter of 0.001 inch. It is used for measuring the cross section of wires.

COAXIAL CABLE.—A transmission line consisting of two conductors concentric with and insulated from each other.

COMMUTATOR.—The copper segments on the armature of a motor or generator. It is cylindrical in shape and is used to pass power into or from the brushes. It is a switching device.

CONDUCTANCE.—The ability of a material to conduct or carry an electric current. It is the reciprocal of the resistance of the material, and is expressed in mhos.

CONDUCTIVITY.—The ease with which a substance transmits electricity.

CONDUCTOR.—Any material suitable for carrying electric current.

CORE.—A magnetic material that affords an easy path for magnetic flux lines in a coil.

COUNTER E.M.F.—Counter electromotive force; an e.m.f. induced in a coil or armature that opposes the applied voltage.

CURRENT LIMITER.—A protective device similar to a fuse, usually used in high amperage circuits.

CYCLE.—One complete positive and one complete negative alternation of a current or voltage.

DIELECTRIC.—An insulator; a term that refers to the insulating material between the plates of a capacitor.

ELECTRICAL TERMS AND FORMULAS

DIODE.—Vacuum tube—a two element tube that contains a cathode and plate; semiconductor—a material of either germanium or silicon that is manufactured to allow current to flow in only one direction. Diodes are used as rectifiers and detectors.

DIRECT CURRENT.—An electric current that flows in one direction only.

EDDY CURRENT.—Induced circulating currents in a conducting material that are caused by a varying magnetic field.

EFFICIENCY.—The ratio of output power to input power, generally expressed as a percentage.

ELECTROLYTE.—A solution of a substance which is capable of conducting electricity. An electrolyte may be in the form of either a liquid or a paste.

ELECTROMAGNET.—A magnet made by passing current through a coil of wire wound on a soft iron core.

ELECTROMOTIVE FORCE (e.m.f.).—The force that produces an electric current in a circuit.

ELECTRON.—A negatively charged particle of matter.

ENERGY.—The ability or capacity to do work.

FARAD.—The unit of capacitance.

FEEDBACK.—A transfer of energy from the output circuit of a device back to its input.

FIELD.—The space containing electric or magnetic lines of force.

FIELD WINDING.—The coil used to provide the magnetizing force in motors and generators.

FLUX FIELD.—All electric or magnetic lines of force in a given region.

FREE ELECTRONS.—Electrons which are loosely held and consequently tend to move at random among the atoms of the material.

FREQUENCY.—The number of complete cycles per second existing in any form of wave motion; such as the number of cycles per second of an alternating current.

FULL-WAVE RECTIFIER CIRCUIT.—A circuit which utilizes both the positive and the negative alternations of an alternating current to produce a direct current.

FUSE.—A protective device inserted in series with a circuit. It contains a metal that will melt or break when current is increased beyond a specific value for a definite period of time.

GAIN.—The ratio of the output power, voltage, or current to the input power, voltage, or current, respectively.

GALVANOMETER.—An instrument used to measure small d-c currents.

GENERATOR.—A machine that converts mechanical energy into electrical energy.

GROUND.—A metallic connection with the earth to establish ground potential. Also, a common return to a point of zero potential. The chassis of a receiver or a transmitter is sometimes the common return, and therefore the ground of the unit.

HENRY.—The basic unit of inductance.

HORSEPOWER.—The English unit of power, equal to work done at the rate of 550 foot-pounds per second. Equal to 746 watts of electrical power.

HYSTERESIS.—A lagging of the magnetic flux in a magnetic material behind the magnetizing force which is producing it.

IMPEDANCE.—The total opposition offered to the flow of an alternating current. It may consist of any combination of resistance, inductive reactance, and capacitive reactance.

INDUCTANCE.—The property of a circuit which tends to oppose a change in the existing current.

INDUCTION.—The act or process of producing voltage by the relative motion of a magnetic field across a conductor.

INDUCTIVE REACTANCE.—The opposition to the flow of alternating or pulsating current caused by the inductance of a circuit. It is measured in ohms.

INPHASE.—Applied to the condition that exists when two waves of the same frequency pass through their maximum and minimum values of like polarity at the same instant.

INVERSELY.—Inverted or reversed in position or relationship.

ISOGONIC LINE.—An imaginary line drawn through points on the earth's surface where the magnetic deviation is equal.

JOULE.—A unit of energy or work. A joule of energy is liberated by one ampere flowing for one second through a resistance of one ohm.

KILO.—A prefix meaning 1,000.

LAG.—The amount one wave is behind another in time; expressed in electrical degrees.

LAMINATED CORE.—A core built up from thin sheets of metal and used in transformers and relays.

LEAD.—The opposite of LAG. Also, a wire or connection.

ELECTRICAL TERMS AND FORMULAS

LINE OF FORCE.—A line in an electric or magnetic field that shows the direction of the force.

LOAD.—The power that is being delivered by any power producing device. The equipment that uses the power from the power producing device.

MAGNETIC AMPLIFIER.—A saturable reactor type device that is used in a circuit to amplify or control.

MAGNETIC CIRCUIT.—The complete path of magnetic lines of force.

MAGNETIC FIELD.—The space in which a magnetic force exists.

MAGNETIC FLUX.—The total number of lines of force issuing from a pole of a magnet.

MAGNETIZE.—To convert a material into a magnet by causing the molecules to rearrange.

MAGNETO.—A generator which produces alternating current and has a permanent magnet as its field.

MEGGER.—A test instrument used to measure insulation resistance and other high resistances. It is a portable hand operated d-c generator used as an ohmmeter.

MEGOHM.—A million ohms.

MICRO.—A prefix meaning one-millionth.

MILLI.—A prefix meaning one-thousandth.

MILLIAMMETER.—An ammeter that measures current in thousandths of an ampere.

MOTOR-GENERATOR.—A motor and a generator with a common shaft used to convert line voltages to other voltages or frequencies.

MUTUAL INDUCTANCE.—A circuit property existing when the relative position of two inductors causes the magnetic lines of force from one to link with the turns of the other.

NEGATIVE CHARGE.—The electrical charge carried by a body which has an excess of electrons.

NEUTRON.—A particle having the weight of a proton but carrying no electric charge. It is located in the nucleus of an atom.

NUCLEUS.—The central part of an atom that is mainly comprised of protons and neutrons. It is the part of the atom that has the most mass.

NULL.—Zero.

OHM.—The unit of electrical resistance.

OHMMETER.—An instrument for directly measuring resistance in ohms.

OVERLOAD.—A load greater than the rated load of an electrical device.

PERMALLOY.—An alloy of nickel and iron having an abnormally high magnetic permeability.

PERMEABILITY.—A measure of the ease with which magnetic lines of force can flow through a material as compared to air.

PHASE DIFFERENCE.—The time in electrical degrees by which one wave leads or lags another.

POLARITY.—The character of having magnetic poles, or electric charges.

POLE.—The section of a magnet where the flux lines are concentrated; also where they enter and leave the magnet. An electrode of a battery.

POLYPHASE.—A circuit that utilizes more than one phase of alternating current.

POSITIVE CHARGE.—The electrical charge carried by a body which has become deficient in electrons.

POTENTIAL.—The amount of charge held by a body as compared to another point or body. Usually measured in volts.

POTENTIOMETER.—A variable voltage divider; a resistor which has a variable contact arm so that any portion of the potential applied between its ends may be selected.

POWER.—The rate of doing work or the rate of expending energy. The unit of electrical power is the watt.

POWER FACTOR.—The ratio of the actual power of an alternating or pulsating current, as measured by a wattmeter, to the apparent power, as indicated by ammeter and voltmeter readings. The power factor of an inductor, capacitor, or insulator is an expression of their losses.

PRIME MOVER.—The source of mechanical power used to drive the rotor of a generator.

PROTON.—A positively charged particle in the nucleus of an atom.

RATIO.—The value obtained by dividing one number by another, indicating their relative proportions.

REACTANCE.—The opposition offered to the flow of an alternating current by the inductance, capacitance, or both, in any circuit.

RECTIFIERS.—Devices used to change alternating current to unidirectional current. These may be vacuum tubes, semiconductors such as germanium and silicon, and dry-disk rectifiers such as selenium and copperoxide.

RELAY.—An electromechanical switching device that can be used as a remote control.

RELUCTANCE.—A measure of the opposition that a material offers to magnetic lines of force.

RESISTANCE.—The opposition to the flow of current caused by the nature and physical dimensions of a conductor.

RESISTOR.—A circuit element whose chief characteristic is resistance; used to oppose the flow of current.

ELECTRICAL TERMS AND FORMULAS

RETENTIVITY. – The measure of the ability of a material to hold its magnetism.

RHEOSTAT. – A variable resistor.

SATURABLE REACTOR. – A control device that uses a small d-c current to control a large a-c current by controlling core flux density.

SATURATION. – The condition existing in any circuit when an increase in the driving signal produces no further change in the resultant effect.

SELF-INDUCTION. – The process by which a circuit induces an e.m.f. into itself by its own magnetic field.

SERIES-WOUND. – A motor or generator in which the armature is wired in series with the field winding.

SERVO. – A device used to convert a small movement into one of greater movement or force.

SERVOMECHANISM. – A closed-loop system that produces a force to position an object in accordance with the information that originates at the input.

SOLENOID. – An electromagnetic coil that contains a movable plunger.

SPACE CHARGE. – The cloud of electrons existing in the space between the cathode and plate in a vacuum tube, formed by the electrons emitted from the cathode in excess of those immediately attracted to the plate.

SPECIFIC GRAVITY – The ratio between the density of a substance and that of pure water, at a given temperature.

SYNCHROSCOPE – An instrument used to indicate a difference in frequency between two a-c sources.

SYNCHRO SYSTEM. – An electrical system that gives remote indications or control by means of self-synchronizing motors.

TACHOMETER. – An instrument for indicating revolutions per minute.

TERTIARY WINDING. – A third winding on a transformer or magnetic amplifier that is used as a second control winding.

THERMISTOR. – A resistor that is used to compensate for temperature variations in a circuit.

THERMOCOUPLE. – A junction of two dissimilar metals that produces a voltage when heated.

TORQUE. – The turning effort or twist which a shaft sustains when transmitting power.

TRANSFORMER. – A device composed of two or more coils, linked by magnetic lines of force, used to transfer energy from one circuit to another.

TRANSMISSION LINES. – Any conductor or system of conductors used to carry electrical energy from its source to a load.

VARS. – Abbreviation for volt-ampere, reactive.

VECTOR. – A line used to represent both direction and magnitude.

VOLT. – The unit of electrical potential.

VOLTMETER. – An instrument designed to measure a difference in electrical potential, in volts.

WATT. – The unit of electrical power.

WATTMETER. – An instrument for measuring electrical power in watts.

Formulas

Ohm's Law for d-c Circuits

$$I = \frac{E}{R} = \frac{P}{E} = \sqrt{\frac{P}{R}}$$

$$R = \frac{E}{I} = \frac{P}{I^2} = \frac{E^2}{P}$$

$$E = IR = \frac{P}{I} = \sqrt{PR}$$

$$P = EI = \frac{E^2}{R} = I^2 R$$

Resistors in Series

$$R_T = R_1 + R_2 \ldots$$

Resistors in Parallel
Two resistors

$$R_T = \frac{R_1 R_2}{R_1 + R_2}$$

More than two

$$\frac{1}{R_T} = \frac{1}{R_1} + \frac{1}{R_2} + \frac{1}{R_3}$$

ELECTRICAL TERMS AND FORMULAS

R-L Circuit Time Constant equals
$\frac{L \text{ (in henrys)}}{R \text{ (in ohms)}} = t$ (in seconds), or

$\frac{L \text{ (in microhenrys)}}{R \text{ (in ohms)}} = t$ (in microseconds)

R-C Circuit Time Constant equals
R (ohms) X C (farads) = t (seconds)
R (megohms) x C (microfarads) = t (seconds)
R (ohms) x C (microfarads) = t (microseconds)
R (megohms) x C (micromicrofrads = t (microseconds)

Comparison of Units in Electric and Magnetic Circuits.

	Electric circuit	Magnetic circuit
Force	Volt, E or e.m.f.	Gilberts, F, or m.m.f.
Flow	Ampere, I	Flux, Φ, in maxwells
Opposition	Ohms, R	Reluctance, R
Law	Ohm's law, $I = \frac{E}{R}$	Rowland's law $\Phi = \frac{F}{R}$
Intensity of force	Volts per cm. of length	$H = \frac{1.257 IN}{L}$, gilberts per centimeter of length
Density	Current density— for example, amperes per cm^2.	Flux density—for example, lines per cm^2., or gausses

Capacitors in Series
Two capacitors
$$C_T = \frac{C_1 C_2}{C_1 + C_2}$$

More than two
$$\frac{1}{C_T} = \frac{1}{C_1} + \frac{1}{C_2} + \frac{1}{C_3}\ldots$$

Capacitors in Parallel
$$C_T = C_1 + C_2 \ldots$$

Capacitive Reactance
$$X_c = \frac{1}{2\pi f C}$$

Impedance in an R-C Circuit (Series)
$$Z = \sqrt{R^2 + X_c^2}$$

Inductors in Series
$L_T = L_1 + L_2 \ldots$ (No coupling between coils)

Inductors in Parallel
Two inductors
$$L_T = \frac{L_1 L_2}{L_1 + L_2}$$ (No coupling between coils)

More than two
$$\frac{1}{L_T} = \frac{1}{L_1} + \frac{1}{L_2} + \frac{1}{L_3} \ldots$$ (No coupling between coils)

Inductive Reactance
$$X_L = 2\pi f L$$

Q of a Coil
$$Q = \frac{X_L}{R}$$

Impedance of an R-L Circuit (series)
$$Z = \sqrt{R^2 + X_L^2}$$

Impedance with R, C, and L in Series
$$Z = \sqrt{R^2 + (X_L - X_C)^2}$$

Parallel Circuit Impedance
$$Z = \frac{Z_1 Z_2}{Z_1 + Z_2}$$

Sine-Wave Voltage Relationships
Average value
$$E_{ave} = \frac{2}{\pi} \times E_{max} = 0.637 E_{max}$$

ELECTRICAL TERMS AND FORMULAS

Effective or r.m.s. value

$$E_{eff} = \frac{E_{max}}{\sqrt{2}} = \frac{E_{max}}{1.414} = 0.707 E_{max} = 1.11 E_{ave}$$

Maximum value

$$E_{max} = \sqrt{2} E_{eff} = 1.414 E_{eff} = 1.57 E_{ave}$$

Voltage in an a-c circuit

$$E = IZ = \frac{P}{I \times P.F.}$$

Current in an a-c circuit

$$I = \frac{E}{Z} = \frac{P}{E \times P.F.}$$

Power in A-C Circuit
Apparent power = EI
True power

$$P = EI \cos \theta = EI \times P.F.$$

Power factor

$$P.F. = \frac{P}{EI} = \cos \theta$$

$$\cos \theta = \frac{\text{true power}}{\text{apparent power}}$$

Transformers
Voltage relationship

$$\frac{E}{E} = \frac{N}{N} \text{ or } E = E \times \frac{N}{N}$$

Current relationship

$$\frac{I_p}{I_s} = \frac{N_s}{N_p}$$

Induced voltage

$$E_{eff} = 4.44 BAfN 10^{-8}$$

Turns ratio equals

$$\frac{N_p}{N_s} = \sqrt{\frac{Z_p}{Z_s}}$$

Secondary current

$$I_s = I_p \frac{N_p}{N_s}$$

Secondary voltage

$$E_s = E_p \frac{N_s}{N_p}$$

Three Phase Voltage and Current Relationships
With wye connected windings

$$E_{line} = 1.732 E_{coil} = \sqrt{3} E_{coil}$$

$$I_{line} = I_{coil}$$

With delta connected windings

$$E_{line} = E_{coil}$$

$$I_{line} = 1.732 I_{coil}$$

With wye or delta connected winding

$$P_{coil} = E_{coil} I_{coil}$$

$$P_t = 3 P_{coil}$$

$$P_t = 1.732 E_{line} I_{line}$$

(To convert to true power multiply by $\cos \theta$)

Synchronous Speed of Motor

$$r.p.m. = \frac{120 \times \text{frequency}}{\text{number of poles}}$$

GREEK ALPHABET

Name	Capital	Lower Case	Designates
Alpha	A	α	Angles.
Beta	B	β	Angles, flux density.
Gamma	Γ	γ	Conductivity.
Delta	Δ	δ	Variation of a quantity, increment.
Epsilon	E	ε	Base of natural logarithms (2.71828).
Zeta	Z	ζ	Impedance, coefficients, coordinates.
Eta	H	η	Hysteresis coefficient, efficiency, magnetizing force.
Theta	Θ	θ	Phase angle.
Iota	I	ι	
Kappa	K	κ	Dielectric constant, coupling coefficient, susceptibility.
Lambda	Λ	λ	Wavelength.
Mu	M	μ	Permeability, micro, amplification factor.
Nu	N	ν	Reluctivity.
Xi	Ξ	ξ	
Omicron	O	o	
Pi	Π	π	3.1416
Rho	P	ρ	Resistivity.
Sigma	Σ	σ	
Tau	T	τ	Time constant, time-phase displacement.
Upsilon	Υ	υ	
Phi	Φ	φ	Angles, magnetic flux.
Chi	X	χ	
Psi	Ψ	ψ	Dielectric flux, phase difference.
Omega	Ω	ω	Ohms (capital), angular velocity ($2\pi f$).

COMMON ABBREVIATIONS AND LETTER SYMBOLS

Term	Abbreviation or Symbol
alternating current (noun)	a.c.
alternating-current (adj.)	a-c
ampere	a.
area	A
audiofrequency (noun)	AF
audiofrequency (adj.)	A-F
capacitance	C
capacitive reactance	X_C
centimeter	cm.
conductance	G
coulomb	Q
counterelectromotive force	c.e.m.f.
current (d-c or r.m.s. value)	I
current (instantaneous value)	i
cycles per second	c.p.s.
dielectric constant	K,k
difference in potential (d-c or r.m.s. value)	E
difference in potential (instantaneous value)	e
direct current (noun)	d.c.
direct-current (adj.)	d-c
electromotive force	e.m.f.
frequency	f
henry	h.
horsepower	hp.
impedance	Z
inductance	L
inductive reactance	X_L
kilovolt	kv.
kilovolt-ampere	kv.-a.
kilowatt	kw.
kilowatt-hour	kw.-hr.
magnetic field intensity	H
magnetomotive force	m.m.f.
megohm	M
microampere	μ a.
microfarad	μ f.
microhenry	μ h.
micromicrofarad	$\mu\mu$ f.
microvolt	μ v.
milliampere	ma.
millihenry	mh.
milliwatt	mw.
mutual inductance	M
power	P
resistance	R
revolutions per minute	r.p.m.
root mean square	r.m.s.
time	t
torque	T
volt	v.
watt	w.

www.ingramcontent.com/pod-product-compliance
Lightning Source LLC
Chambersburg PA
CBHW081829300426
44116CB00014B/2518